PLANET TWO

Other books by Lynn Grabhorn

Excuse Me, Your Life Is Waiting

The Excuse Me, Your Life Is Waiting *Playbook*

Dear God! What's Happening to Us?

Beyond the Twelve Steps

PLANET TWO

Earth in a Higher Dimension . . .

Are You Ready?

lynn grabhorn

HAMPTON ROADS
PUBLISHING COMPANY, INC.

Cover design by Jane Hagaman
Cover photos copyright © 2003 Comstock Images
www.comstock.com

Hampton Roads Publishing Company, Inc.
1125 Stoney Ridge Road
Charlottesville, VA 22902

434-296-2772
fax: 434-296-5096
e-mail: hrpc@hrpub. com
www. hrpub. com

If you are unable to order this book from your local
bookseller, you may order directly from the publisher.
Call 1-800-766-8009, toll-free.

Library of Congress Cataloging-in-Publication Data

Grabhorn, Lynn
  Planet two : Earth in a higher frequency : are you ready? / Lynn
Grabhorn.
      p. cm.
  ISBN 1-57174-407-X (5-1/2x8-1/2 : alk. paper)
  1. Spiritual life--Miscellanea. I. Title.
  BF1999.G678 2004
  133.9--dc22
                                              2003021782

10 9 8 7 6 5 4 3 2 1

Printed on acid-free paper in Canada

table
of
contents

Planet Two

introduction

Webster says a trilogy is three books that, although individually complete, are closely related in theme.

If I had had any idea that I was going to be doing a trilogy of books related to . . . well, let's see . . . related to what? Our own betterment? Cosmic law? How to make a new life both here and *where?* You can bet I would have passed. Quickly!

Excuse Me, Your Life Is Waiting, and *Dear God! What's Happening to Us?* were the first two books of this trilogy, though I never knew that until this one came along. (Yes, I wrote *Beyond the Twelve Steps* and I still love it, but it's not part of this trilogy.)

Planet Two is the last, but by no means the least important in this trilogy. Now that this book is finished, here's how I see it:

Dear God . . . I'm So Sorry!

All the way through this book, you'll find this: (see *Dear God* . . .) to the point where you'll undoubtedly want to scream. I can only tell you that if you haven't read *Dear God* . . . you'll be quite lost in reading this.

I had no idea after *Excuse Me* . . .that there was more coming. And I had no idea when I wrote *Dear God* . . . that there was more coming.

I guess that *Excuse Me* . . . was put on the front burner to become a best seller, and be on the *New York Times* best-seller list just to grease the slide, so to speak. (Many e-mailers have told me that if it hadn't been for *Excuse Me* . . . they would never have purchased *Dear God* . . . Ah, those grand cosmic schemes!)

In other words, "Get folks believing in you, Lynn, and they'll buy the other two, which are both as necessary to our plan as *Excuse Me* . . . has been."

The troops of the cosmos are never beyond deception if it will accomplish what they want. In this case, they wanted to make sure that *Dear God* . . . would have a large audience, which surely would never have happened if it had come out first as a solo from an unknown author.

Where I'm going with this is . . . I beg you . . . before you read this book, please, please, *please* read *Dear God* . . . (You can get it from the publisher for 30 percent off, or from Amazon.com for almost that same discount! See lynngrabhorn.com web site.) Without reading that short book, there's far too much in this one that will make no sense at all.

Damn it, I'm really sorry to sound like an advertising agent, but the importance of that book is beyond description, not just to your understanding of what's in *this* book, but to your Life!

What Folks Have Asked Me

The e-mails and testimonials have been pouring in about *Dear God* . . . but apparently I didn't answer some important questions that folks have had. Those same questions have been repeated in just about every other e-mail.

1) *How many times do I have to say the statements?*

Just once. Your guides have been waiting for you to spit these out and are ready to make the necessary changes. Those changes may take a few weeks, or, they could be instantaneous (as many have told me). Just do them, and don't worry about "Now?" "Later?" or "When?"

2) *May I put the statements in my own words?*

At first I answered, "Yes, of course," but didn't check

it out. I'm told now, "No, no! Only in the words we gave you that are in the book."

3) *What about the grid and portals you mention. Is it just for the planet we're on now?*

No. The one hundred or so people who are mentioned in the Epilogue of *Dear God . . .* are now doing their work only for Planet Two to create portals between here and there, in order for people to leave as easily and smoothly as possible for that planet. Sort of like the making of a bunch of high frequency portals for us to slip through, and a high frequency grid that will restrict The Others from entering.

There will be many more doing this work. It's not fun (I'm doing it now), but hang in there . . . take something for depression . . . and just know that what you are doing—if you are doing it—is *beyond all measure of importance* for the Light. I wish you well!

4) *If I take the steps in* Dear God . . . *will it apply to my youngsters also?*

Yes, but only up to about age four. Past that, they're going to have to get it on their own or from you eventually.

5) Nothing of this next piece was in the *Dear God . . .* book, but I've been asked to relay it to you. If you have a dear relative in a nursing home who

wants out, as so many do, type up the statements for them to read. For heaven's sake, don't give them the book . . . just the statements, large enough so they can read them and then say out loud someplace. I'm told that many who read the statements will transition very soon after that. But please don't holler at me if they don't.

By the way, this is *only* for those in nursing homes; not just sick, or terminally ill, or just tired of life.

The 1-2-3-3 ½ Punch

Okay, enough on *Dear God* . . . Here's how it needs to come down for all of us with this trilogy of books.

1) I have to presume you've read *Excuse Me* . . . If not, please get it.

2) Then, *Dear God* . . .

3) Then, *Planet Two*

—and then—

3½) As soon as you can, dive into the *Excuse Me* . . . *Playbook*. I had so much fun putting it together, but of course, had no idea at the time it would be used to help folks get to Planet Two. Well, now you know. And please, don't skimp!

Where All This Came From

I'm told that this is the end as far as more books are concerned. Man, I hope so! Getting this information is not the easiest thing to do. And you might like to know how this happens, meaning, how I get it.

If you've read *Dear God* . . . you know it's channeled and how I do it. I "hear" an answer, or a pushy kind of thought in my head (meaning "Hey. . . listen up. . . we want you to get this down"). Maybe I've asked, "Is it this way, or is that how it really happens?" etc.

Then I confirm it with my swinger (made out of a six inch string, a half-inch driveway rock, and glue!)—and keep at it until I've confirmed I'm getting the proper answer, which is usually not very long since I've already been "downloaded" with they want me to write.

Who are "they"? Well, it really doesn't make any difference, except to say that they are of the highest— can't get any higher—reality/dimension/frequency of Light. I now truly trust what's coming through—most of the time. Sometimes "the guys" will mess around with me to suit their needs, but never when writing a book.

How do I know this? Gosh, I wish I could tell you. I just know. At times I curse them. Other times, I giggle with them, and still other times I make fun of them. But I always, always know that when it comes to writing these books, it's right on. Never any messing around, unless there's something they just flat out don't want me to know.

A Couple of Things . . .

You'll notice that the word "god" in this book is not capitalized. Please try not to be offended by that. I was clearly told to do it that way, except as part of the title in *Dear God . . .*

You'll also notice that reference to "The Others" is also capitalized. This has nothing to do with reverence or honor, only to set those more common words apart.

What's This Book About?

About 80 percent of the information in this book has never been released before, much like *Dear God . . .* I'm not at all sure I enjoy the position of getting it out there, but that's the way it is.

This book is about what's available to us after we leave here (meaning "die" to this reality). Most of it is information I have not known before and is fascinating beyond words.

If you believe it, fine. If you don't, then, so be it. S'okay with me, but might not be okay with you in times to come.

At any rate, this is a fun, amazing, happy, and deeply moving story, which I believe to be fully true. It's the book that fills in the pieces and plugs the holes between the other two. However, judge for yourself . . . paradise or fantasy.

In joy!! And, enjoy!

Lynn Grabhorn

chapter one

what, why,
where, when

While there may have been other books written about this little-known planet, the only one I've come across was written by Machaelle Small Wright, called *Dancing in the Shadows of the Moon*.[1] (Amazon.com has it.)

And, while there's precious little in her book about this wondrously amazing and challenging place we're calling Planet Two (no, not Planet "X"), I seem to have locked onto this arena like a shark onto its quarry.

Yes, there are references to this way of life in the Bible, though I have no idea where. This just comes from e-mails I've received.

And yes, I know that many great masters, and psychics,

---

[1] Wright, M. S., *Dancing in the Shadows of the Moon* (Perelandra, Ltd., PO Box 3603, Warrenton, VA 22186, 1995).

and oracles have talked about this unseen location for centuries, always without naming it. But since I can't relate to stuff that is not described in the simplest of human terms, I've never paid much attention to anything that was said about this apparent heaven-on-Earth, until Machaelle's book came out.

Machaelle is so "normal," she squeaks of everyday human. That sold me, and from then on I spent countless hours trying to find out all I could about this Earth Planet Two, but my cosmic troops weren't talking. I guess they wanted me to get *Dear God* . . . out first, then they'd lay it on me. And oh man alive, have they ever!

Most of what I first knew about Planet Two is in *Dear God* . . . Not a whole lot of scintillating information, yet enough to keep me very turned-on about mankind's future (and for sure, about mine as well).

So here we go . . .
what is this place . . . ?
why is it . . . ?
where is it . . . ?
when did it all start . . . ?
and how come it's so important to you and
 me? Or is it?
And how come we haven't known about it
 forever on a "take it for granted" basis,
 like Mars is here, Venus is there, etc.?
And who really cares anyhow?

Just Another Ho-Hum Planet?

Not hardly. In brief, Planet Two is a duplicate of Earth. In fact, it *is* Earth, just in a higher dimension, which means it vibrates faster than our eyes can see, like a whirling fan.

Planet Two is populated with humans of two different dimensions, and, except for a few wonder of wonders, we'd be hard pressed to tell it apart from our Earth where we live now. But of course, those "few wonders" are gigantic (and then some!).

First: Planet Two is relatively pristine, about 80 percent cleaner and fresher than we are. Their lakes and rivers are unpolluted; their rain forests still stand; their ozone layer is fully intact and harmful radiation from the sun is minimal. Yes, logging in some forests has been a bit of a problem, but that's being taken care of.

Second: Planet Two has far fewer people, which I'd call a major biggie. While it has only about twenty million people on it now, it will never have more than somewhere around a billion people populating its whole beautiful sphere. Compare that to our—what is it now?—around seven billion? Wow! Serious room to spread out and breathe on Planet Two.

Third: and maybe most important of all: The
influence of the dark, or The Others, those of a
low frequency who have been screwing around
with us here on this Earth for far too many eons
and messing up our lives big time, will be reduced
by about 80 percent. They'll still be hanging
around there for a while—like about 200 years or
so—but will gradually be booted out of there, one
way or another. And then? Well, I can hardly
imagine! But for now, we'll just stick with the first
couple of hundred years.

The Three Earths

There are really three Earths which we're calling
Planet One, Planet Two, and Planet Three. And, hold on
to your hats: they were all formed as spin offs from
Jupiter, pretty much at the same time. (Oh boy, I can hear
the scientists and astronomers screaming now, "How do
you know that? We don't believe anything of the sort.
What proof do you have? How *dare* you!")

Sorry guys, I have no proof, only Machaelle's book.
However, it's been known for some time by those who
have attended classes of gifted esoteric teachers that
Jupiter is where our planet came from, as well as the
other two Earths, which no one has ever much talked
about.

Frankly, it's not an altogether pretty story, and the full

escapade is far too long and involved to be detailed here (see *Dear God . . .*) nonetheless, here are a few of the pertinent details.

Planet One (that's us!), Part I

Planet One, our present Earth, was spun off to be an exciting new kind of vacation spot for the lower dimension experimental beings the Jupiter scientists had created. They looked much like what we call "cavemen." (From here on in, I'll just call the Jupiter guys the "J's.")

Oh, by the way, the experimental beings they created are now called humans!

Because the J's were of the eighth dimension, and not physical, which is what they were after, they decided to stock this new amusement park with all manner of outlandish creatures that might give their experimental, physical beings something to get excited about. (It got them excited, all right!)

The entire vacation planet was created in the third dimension, since that's the same dimension in which the J's had created their cute little cloned experiments. They were exploring physicality, and third dimension gave it to them. They could have gone to even the seventh dimension for physicality, but third was their choice at the time, sort of like starting from the bottom up. And they

5

knew that the third would easily hold any other kind of mass for their new planet, such as trees, water, etc.

There was, at that time on Jupiter, a very small group who could create by thought alone, and they were the ones doing all this new-planet building. Since the third dimensional pride they had created (Planet One) was for study and examination of the new third dimensional clones, and was wrapped in the guise of a vacation spot, they somehow concocted greenery and waters all around for some of their *other* creations.

These were not warm, fuzzy, cuddly little things, but creatures that the J's had conjured up to give their third dimensional experiments a thrill. Like dinosaurs, large and small, with wings and without, and of every possible description. It was sort of a contest to see who could make the most terrifying creatures. Seems to me they got stuck in a rut with lizard-type stuff. Oh well.

But there was something else happening which the J's were unprepared for. Just like the very best of science fiction, their planet was being attacked by powerful and unknown energies from an unknown source. As advanced as they were, they knew that unless these energies abated, they would be wiped out. And so plans were laid to remove themselves from their home planet as soon as possible.

Planet Two: Part I

Planet Two is a planet of sixth dimensional frequency. Most of the entities who live there now are of the sixth dimension, and of course, quite human.

The J's hadn't used Planet Two yet for their experiments with physical bodies, so it wasn't known how sixth dimension would work. But third dimension was working nicely on Planet One, and soon they'd start to work with Planet Two. Only they never got the chance, at least not by choice.

The problem these guys faced, since they were most surely not physical and could not just transfer as higher dimensional Light bodies to any of these planets to be saved from the invading cosmic energies, was how to maintain their species.

(Man! What a science fiction story! Only it's not fiction!)

How could they hold on to all that they had created over countless eons of development? The number of places throughout the universe where they might be welcomed was zero. Barren, unused planets that would be of a proper vibrational frequency for them were so hostile to their species, going to any one of them would be exceptionally strenuous. Their situation was becoming desperate, and the energies were getting worse.

Planet Two

**(I need to tell you now that their species,
the J's, were not, and are not, of the Light.
They were the prime force of
The Others within this universe.)**

Planet Three: Part I

We'll call the small (and very odd) group I mentioned that had hatched these planets, The Thinkers, because that's all they did. They were created by the J's to do more, make more, formulate more, originate and orchestrate more. Their brilliance was unsurpassed throughout the entire universe, except for the one we would call the creator.

While they may have been brilliant beyond all imagination, they were most assuredly not a group of happy campers. They hated their J creators with an unvarnished obsession, though there was not a thing they could do about it. But then the energies came. And The Thinkers knew they would have their day.

Planet Three, also third dimension and of course also created by this odd group of Thinkers, was to be another experimental planet, but was being held in reserve for the time being while they played around with their repugnant animals on Planet One and watched their experimental bodies react in horror.

There were no animals, no greens, and no waters on

8

Planet Three. It was simply what you would call your basically unfriendly environment. No one had been sent there yet, but the J's thought that in time, this would be a grand place to do more experiments with their third dimensional creations.

No entities of the dark were of a higher dimension than eighth dimension. (Planets with beings of 100 percent Light reach much higher dimensions.) The whole purpose of the original experiments by the J's was to slowly build a different form for themselves that would ultimately accept eighth dimension as physical. They never made it. And, they never will.

Then Comes "Oops"

The energetic forces attacking Jupiter were unrelenting and growing stronger. The J's ordered The Thinkers to stop the incoming energies, but The Thinkers, hating their creators, refused. "Let the energies come in and exterminate them all," said The Thinkers. "Let them be destroyed by their own totalitarian madness."

Needless to say, the J's were a wee bit upset with this group, yet there was no time now to do anything about it. They had to get out of there, fast, or they'd be goners.

No need to go into the "whys" of this catastrophic event that happened for the J's and their planet, or we'd be into a whole separate book. Let's just say that the Light was at work . . . overtime! (And who knows how much involvement The Thinkers might have had.)

Helplessness seemed to be the feeling of the day, not to mention abject terror. Oh yes, the J's surely knew they had to leave, but how? And to where? Being of The Others, where would they be welcomed?

Well, about 75 percent of them ventured back to their homes *outside* of this universe, which is totally of the dark. As for the remaining bunch, some decided to begin new activities on uninhabited planets that would hold their frequencies. While there may be only eight or ten of these planets inhabited by The Others today, they've been raising holy hell throughout our entire universe.

Meanwhile "Back at the Ranch . . ."

Then came a gargantuan decision for those who did not want to go back home, outside of this universe. They had found something within this universe they wanted to chase and be a part of (called Light and on-going Life), and were willing to put their lives on the line to see if they could achieve it through these new lower dimensional bodies.

"What if we put ourselves into these bodies, and went to one of our new planets?"

The most courageous of them decided to risk it, but they also knew they had to get Planet One (ours) away from their home planet and the destructive energies. If they didn't, *bye bye.*

And so, having no idea that The Thinkers were planning on getting into bodies themselves, the J's went crawling to them for help, asking that the planet they intended to inhabit be moved to another part of the universe, and even another solar system.

But the odd ones said, "Sorry, you creators of horrors; you're on your own. We are going to inhabit some of the bodies you've created and move these planets away, but not that far away. If some of you want to come along, then get into the bodies."

The Thinkers had found a way of moving these three little planets out of Jupiter's orbit. Yes, it was a risk for them, but anything would be better than the incomprehensible slavery of around-the-clock thinking. And so The Thinkers were more than willing to take their chances on entering bodies on any of these planets. After the hell in which they'd been incarcerated, nothing could be worse.

"Please!! Where Are We Going?"

The thousand or so J's who decided to enter the

cloned bodies had no idea where they were going, or how long it would take, or if they could survive the journey. Plus, there was no way back, and no way of getting out of their third dimensional bodies once they were in them.

Planet One: Part II

The three Earth planets were now on their way out of the deadly energies attacking Jupiter, and headed toward another part of our solar system. They were coming here, where we are now.

The J's repeatedly asked The Thinkers where they were going, but The Thinkers never replied. And the J's were terrified.

Did destruction lie ahead? Could they survive this transfer of their energies into such a low frequency, not to mention being trapped on a planet of physical mass which they had never experienced before? They had no clue. And they still had the dinosaurs to deal with.

The vacation spot which they had built for their experiments—which they now inhabited—was being rapidly shoved by The Thinkers out of Jupiter's orbit and into a much closer orbit to our sun. It didn't take long before the J's could sense and even see that the closer they got to our sun, the higher the radiation was becoming. Not good news. And The Thinkers weren't saying a thing.

Since the J's—even in their cloned bodies—were so advanced in their technologies and deeply concerned about what the increasing and very unfamiliar radiation would do to their cloned forms, they decided that their only hope of survival was to head for some kind of cover. Not only would this get them away from the increasing strength of the sun's rays, but away from their unfriendly giants who were now becoming meat eaters. What the J's did not know then was that the unaccustomed radiation from our sun, as the planet got closer and closer to it, would cause the dinosaurs to . . . well . . . kick the bucket.

The shelter the J's chose to concoct was underground where they constructed a makeshift world that lasted them for several centuries. (Scientists know where the entrance to this underground world is, but for whatever reason, no one's talking.)

Then, after about a decade when this small group had burrowed out their underground home in which to hide and survive, they finally stuck their noses out and found that not only had the planet's journey been completed, but their tall and big-mouthed adversaries were gone. Their new home, our Earth, was now in the exact same orbit around the sun that we are now, just as it's been for eons, and far enough away from the sun to cause no harm from radiation.

After watching all of this unfold, entities of the Light decided they wanted to give this place a try, knowing full well that to do this, they'd have to come into bodies that were of the dark. Still, it sounded like an intriguing adventure to a somewhat old and bored group of the Light.

By now, the undergrounders were procreating nicely, and some of the big bosses of The Others agreed to let entities of the Light become involved—*slowly*. So they did, and it wasn't long before the majority of the undergrounders, including The Thinkers, had at least *some* Light within them. Since The Others were trying to acquire what the Light offered, this seemed an ideal arrangement to them.

With most of the creatures above ground now gone, leaving only a few of the smaller species and some very strange birds, it was time to come out of hiding.

Now their population started to *really* grow as more and more entities of the Light wanted to give this third dimensional gig a whirl, and were happily popping into bodies that were becoming an interesting mix of Light and dark, though still primarily dark.

Planet Two: Part II

Centuries passed, and civilizations and cultures (of which there have been many we're unaware of) became a basic reality on our planet.

But wouldn't you know, because the planet was almost 90 percent dark, these explorers from the Light found it to be a bit more arduous than they had bargained for. They were trying to contribute and make a difference for the sake of the Light, but frankly the odds were against them. So, they wanted off, and out.

"Sorry guys, you opted for a body and you're stuck with it for a whole bunch more lifetimes until things start to change. We're working on it. Hang on."

The fun and excitement was wearing thin, and the entities of Light felt trapped, caged, and utterly frustrated. After several centuries of this, they started screaming bloody murder to their bosses of Light that they wanted *out*.

Finally, the bosses of Light said to a few of these entities, "Okay, look. There's this other planet Earth which is three dimensions higher from where you are now. It's not as high as where most of you have come from, eighth . . . ninth . . . tenth dimension, but at least you could make a fresh start there without very much interference from The Others. We think we could keep most of them out of there, except the mix that you carry with you now."

The plan was complex, for no humanoid had ever held a frequency much higher than around 70 Megahertz (MHz), which was strictly third dimension.

To be on Planet Two, it was decided that, with some

major adjustments to the whole physical system (the body), and a good bit of time to prepare, a few of these human creatures with souls of the Light could be rewired—while here—for sixth dimension at a frequency well over 200 MHz. This would accomplish two things:

1) By using their human bodies as transducers, it would create a portal between here and there through which the humans who were ready with even slightly higher frequencies could transport, if they so desired, and

2) It would create, for those who were being raised to this high frequency, an assured means to incarnate to that planet, Planet Two.

(I'm really sorry, but no one is telling me why this raising of frequencies to make a portal between realities, and a whole new grid around Planet Two, has to go through humans.)

The process, for those who were being the transducers, was as excruciating then as it is now. (Yes, the same thing is happening again, now, with some people here in preparation for the Birth.) But they stuck with it to help develop this exciting new human body into a higher dimension and a much more enjoyable place to live.

Just as now, the bosses of Light got a bunch of their friends from the Light to agree that after they got into the third dimensional bodies, they would allow themselves to slowly have their frequencies raised in order to have the human form adjust, over time, to a higher vibration. Not fun, I guarantee, but it worked!

The place looked like Earth, it smelled like Earth, but now there was a clean palette for these explorers to paint on. Pristine, empty except for vegetation, and so very ready for crafting.

Because of the planet's higher frequencies and the higher frequency of the reconstructed bodies, The Others ended up with only about 20 percent control rather than the 80 percent they've maintained here.

Why didn't everyone from here want to reincarnate there? Well, after the word got out about this place, most everyone did want to go there, so limits and requirements had to be established. That kept a whole assortment out, as they still held far too much dark.

Life forms of all kinds started to sprout on Planet Two. And of course, with perfect planning, the number of humanoids incarnating there continued to be restricted to only those who held much more Light than dark, even though their Light/dark mix still existed.

It wasn't all that long ago when this . . . well . . . let's call it a migration . . . took place. By the time it actually happened, the human had become a fully recognizable human being, as we have now. And since those who incarnated to Planet Two had all had lives on our planet, and helped to create the types of civilizations we have now, the set up there stayed fairly close to our set up here: culturally, geographically, ethnically, religiously, and so on.

Planet Three: Part II

Once again, in extraordinary and obviously divine planning, it was decided by the bosses of Light that only one planet of third dimension would become their focus for teachings of the Light, teachings that would hopefully help to wake us up. They chose our planet, and had measured success with their plan.

Jesus, Mohammed, Buddha, Zarathustra, along with most of the so-called saints and a lot of other entities were sent here to awaken humanity to its potential. But they were not sent to Planet Three.

Planet Three was basically turned over to the any of the remaining J's throughout our universe who wanted to play around with being in a physical body. So that planet is 100 percent dark. Always has been, always will be. Human, yes, but oh, so dark and so filled with hate and turbulence. I guess there's no real description for it in our terms.

The stage was being set for a universal transformation the likes of which had never been experienced or known. As for the three Earths? Well, in much less than a century, Planet Three will be gone. And so will the planet we're on now.

Heaven on Earth?

What is intended for the enlightened human is Planet Two:

— a place of learning,

— a place of wisdom,

— a place that will still have to deal with The Others for a time,

— a place of incomprehensible beauty (as was ours, once upon a time),

— a place of well-being,

— a place of provocative and thrilling challenges,

— and a place where almost all of mankind gets along.

In time to come, all of mankind *will* get along! Wow!

Where Is It?

Planet Two is in our same vicinity, but totally unseen by most of us because of its higher frequency. There are billions of higher frequency planets, suns, etc. out there that we're incapable of seeing right now. These realities vibrate so much faster than we do, even the strongest

19

telescopes can't pick them up, though a handful of astrologers, clairvoyants, a few psychics have clearly seen this planet. Astrologers have talked about it, and it's been in print—a little bit—but not much.

Let's just put it this way. The existence of Planet Two is somewhat known, but I haven't the foggiest idea where the thing is hiding. I know it's not too far from us, is a bit farther away from the sun than we are, and to our West.

(As for Planet Three . . . it's hidden behind something in our solar system, but that's all I know . . . or care to know.)

Okay: How Come!?

No need to replicate the entire *Dear God . . .* book here, which explains very clearly, "how come this is happening." However, here's a quickie as to "Why," meaning what's the point; what's the purpose? The big question for me when I started finding out about Planet Two was, "Why on Earth haven't we been told about this before? If it's been there all along, and it's a place so many of us are being groomed for, then why has it been such a big secret?!" When I wrote *Dear God . . .* I found out. No entity of the Light, whether a teacher here or in any other reality, has been allowed to talk about the deals that were made with The Others, deals that insured the development of this universe.

Teach all you can about the Light, and about who and

what these humans really are and can become, but keep your silence about the reality of how this universe came to be. This need for silence will soon be lifted. And now it has been.

No entity of the Light who may have come in as pure Light to help with our awakening, and who came in with no mix of the dark that most of humanity still holds, has been allowed to say a word about our association with The Others, or the original agreement between the Light and the dark that involved the entire universe from its inception. They were only barely allowed to talk about what we, as humans, might be able to obtain if we could "find joy." (Man, how I always hated to hear that!)

Until just recently, that agreement of silence has been solemnly adhered to ever since the universe began. It had to be, or else our universe, the only place of Light throughout the entire Isness, would not now exist. But at long last, that agreement is broken. It's in the cosmic garbage can, which is why I'm able to get this information now for both *Dear God . . .* and this book.

Talk about major intrigue! This beats any detective story ever written.

The Critical Human (Who!? Us?)

Countless eons ago, when our universe was first hatching, a plan was set in place by the Light to rid our universe of the influences of The Others who, unfortunately, had to have a major part in our formation. That plan, far older than time itself, is now being enacted, and sure enough, the human is a major player in the overall scheme. It's not that we're any kind of hot-shot species, but the role we're to play in the impending Birth is huge.

Before going on . . . let's take a quick look at this upcoming Birth thing.

The monumental happening of the Birth has been referred to in every religion on the planet, from the arrangement of the Mayan calendar, to the Bible, to the Torah, etc., etc. The fact that there's going to be a major universal event is not big news to religious scholars. They've just never known what it was all about . . . or why. No one has known, until now, that the purpose of this mammoth occurrence was (and is) to rid our universe of the influence of The Others, once and for all. Most of the thousands of different realities in our universe already hold entities of one hundred percent pure Light. So what's the need for this Birth happening, which will take the entire universe to another level?

Why the Birth?

First of all, the Birth will screen out any possibility of new influx from The Others. They'll just have to do their thing outside of our universal womb. That means no more interference—of any kind—in any reality. Not too bad! (Well yes, Planet Two will have some aggravation from The Others for a while, but not for long.)

However, we humans on all three of these earths, are the only realities left that house the dark.

So, to repeat a few facts:

— We house portions of the dark here in our bodies (and in many parts of what we call "heaven") where they can be in minor to major control of what's happening in our lives, and around the worlds.

— Nonetheless, the vast majority of us here are now at least 50 percent Light. (Things are looking up from when we of the Light first jumped into these bodies.)

— Planet Three is entirely dark. Must be a glorious place.

— Planet Two still houses far too much dark, but even so, holds the answer to making this entire universe one of Light.

— We, as humans, are going to assist in the means to universally scrap what remains of the dark into cosmic junk heaps. If we don't, the entire universe will remain affected, and continue to bear the consequences of the dark energies.

The execution of that will be the Birth. Damn soon.

To the Rescue

Believe it or not, at one time it was thought a hopeless task to try to alter this pain-in-the-universal-neck, meaning us. Not that it was our fault, just that the assignment to get us turned around seemed so hopeless. But the bosses of Light came to our rescue and decided to bring as many as possible of us to Planet Two within a certain time frame. There, the transformation of each individual into pure Light—but still remaining physical—could begin to unfold.

Everyone else? Well, Planet Three, as you know, will be obliterated. Those of us here who can't connect with the higher frequencies necessary to make it to Planet Two will probably end up back in their original homes outside of the universe. Sadly, that will entail most of our population.

This universe is going to 100 percent Light, and if we, as humans, don't make it this time, it will be zillions upon zillions of years before another attempt at "Birthing" can be made. I would say, frankly, that "failure is not an option."

This universe is going to 100 percent Light, and each one of us needs to design our own program to get us there.

This universe is going to 100 percent Light. If we want

out of the insanity going on now around the planet, if we want out of tough times, and emotional pain, and stress, and money problems, and everything else that we've been steadfastly going through in our lifetimes, we must find the ways to raise our individual frequencies.

The portals which are being built for us to go through, along with the higher frequency grid around that planet, are almost complete. Only a few other events need to occur, and the Birth will take place.

This universe is going to 100 percent Light, as is Planet Two. Lift off will begin before 2012.

You want to sign up for the ride?

chapter two

living
and dying
where?

The Juicy Stuff

I'm busting at the seams to get into all the neat stuff about Planet Two, like how it operates, who's there, what we'll do there, how long we'll stay, where we'll live, the money system, the governments, who else is coming, etc., etc. Not only do I want to relay all this kicky new material to you, but I want to find it out for myself.

First, though, there's something we just have to get behind us, once and for all time. And that's the matter of so-called death.

You Cannot Die! Period!

In every book I've written, there's been at least a paragraph or two about how death is a cosmic joke, though never in much detail. Other things in the books seemed to be far more important. I hoped that readers would simply accept the truth that there is no such thing as death, except for the body, and let it go at that. Bad idea!

I've seen since in e-mails and letters and seminars, that most folks still have a problem with the concept of "living forever." And I do not mean "eternally at rest," or the usual "he's at peace now," after someone's death. Oh man, quite the contrary. No way!!!

It is totally, utterly, absolutely, incontrovertibly impossible for you to cease existence within this universe, where you'll undoubtedly live for the rest of eternity, if you have even the tiniest spark of Light in you. (And I guarantee, you wouldn't be reading this book unless you did.) I mean . . . it is I-m-p-o-s-s-i-b-l-e! Can't be done! Will never happen!

If you still don't believe that, and if you were in front of me right now, I'd probably lose it and holler, "*No way* can you cease to exist. *No way*! You just can't!" It's a principle of physics, damn it all. Light can never, ever be extinguished (never mind our electric bulbs). Light, that high frequency our universe was created from and which is a part of you, just can not be put out. Not now, not ever. What's it going to take to get this fact accepted? We've been so improperly indoctrinated, because of The Others needing to create fear within us, that even though we *have* been told by some sources that extinction or obliteration was completely impossible by virtue of the Light within us,

which—*can*—*not*—be—extinguished,

Can not be extinguished,

Can . . . not . . . be . . . extinguished.

People are still terrified of death, thanks to the brilliant work of The Others. The Others have seen to it that all mention of so-called reincarnation was removed from the Bible, as well as from the sacred texts of many other religions. Why? Well hell, which created wonderful fear (low frequency vibrations) for The Others to feed off. (Something has to feed every entity that exists. For The Others, it's low frequency.) As long as humans continued to be terrified of death, and to wonder if they were going to go to hell, or oblivion, or wander aimlessly around where they had died and haunt people, they're going to be in for a mean and bumpy ride. Just that fear of death alone will keep their vibrations way too low to accomplish much of anything except trouble.

✧✧✧

(This is way cool!) Entities of the Light say that as far as humans are concerned, the *real* "dying" is coming into a human body. And that the *real* "birthing" is in leaving our bodies, or what we call death. Little wonder entities of the Light think that way; this place has not been exactly gentle or overly nurturing to any of us. Granted, when we leave this reality, we can't just wave a wand and say we want to go into another reality, thereby avoiding coming back to Earth. If we have chosen to become human, we have to finish the whole bloody cycle, but again, that's another book. The dark within us is a part of what we are, and until that's removed (*Dear God . . .* will do it), getting into any other reality is never going to happen. Yes, over the course of the many lifetimes most of us have had here, there were ways to get rid of that mix within us of too-much-dark-with-the-Light, which has caused such horrendous trouble over the centuries. But we can do that now. And oh, how much easier our journey will be when we do.

So, we've been stuck with the humanoid existence, which callously turns out the lights of remembrance when we come in here. Those are the lights that would allow us to know the true Self within us, for if we have any Light at all, we have a soul, and a spirit, and on-going Life. That's what those blasted Others want, but will never, ever get. We can thank The Others for this heartless omission of remembrance. I can assure you, the amnesia of our cosmic origins we all suffer from was not our idea; it was theirs, to create more fear and anxiety, which would always provide more food for them to live off of. Also, so that we would never know how we came to be . . . originally.

The only way I know of avoiding coming back into this not-always-pleasant reality, and to set up something that is damn near 'round the clock pleasure, is to do the simple five minute steps in *Dear God* . . . and then (!) do all you can to live by the tenets in *Excuse Me.* . . . Believe me, I'm not saying this to sell books. As I said before, I don't need to. I was hit in the fanny to write those two books—and now this one—to get as many of us as possible ready to hit the new Earth with both feet running. I don't know about you, but I'm sure as hell ready!

What's It Like?

We've heard it over and over: "Dying is a part of living." Yeah? Well, *wrong,* if dying means extinction, or existing in some sort of never-never land of spirit! Just completely wrong. Crossing over, or transitioning, or passing are more appropriate terms. So, okay, let's get into it.

We have all sorts of physical channels or mediums on TV now who get messages from relatives who have "passed," or "crossed over." Fun media, yes. But real?

Well, yes, it's real . . . *however* . . . there's much, much more to what goes on when we leave here.

First of all though, *what's it like to die*, or terminate the physicality of this life? Considering that I've never done it in this lifetime, I'm sure as hell not speaking from first-hand experience. Some of what I know to be true comes from trusted books and tapes and channeled classes I've attended. The rest has been "downloaded" to me in the last few days, so I could pass it on to both of us.

The amount of Light you've had in your physical "mix" will determine your "after-you're-outta-here" experiences. But of course, first comes the, "Oh Wow, I'm leaving!"

Far and away the best description I've ever read of this experience (and told by my cosmic troops that his description is essentially true for all of us) is the description John Lennon gives in his book, *Peace at Last*,[2] a must-read for anyone still worried about after-death.

As I felt the release of my physical body, I knew it was dead.
A powerful surge of Light filled the room, and the world
I had known disappeared. I was being swept
through a tunnel as bright as the sun itself.

John is talking about that part of death we've all heard about, the tunnel and the bright Light . . . but then what?

---

[2] Leen, Jason, *Peace at Last* (Bellingham, Washington 1989)
Illumination Arts Publishing Company.

"Then what" is basically the same for all of us, except those of more than 50 percent dark. And even if your mix is more than 50 percent dark, you still have that beautiful soul (your memory bank or hard drive), no matter how heavy your "mix" of the dark may be.

Before we go on, I want you to know why I'm bringing this up. After all, if we're going to take our body with us through a portal to another dimension of Earth, why worry about the "normal" death experience? Okay, fair question.

It's because this biggest of fears has to get put behind us, shaken off, terminated . . . permanently.

So:

— if we're concerned that we might not make it to Planet Two, then let's at least dump any other fears still hanging around about so-called "normal" death.

— that way, once that fear of death is dumped, we don't need to be concerned about any of this dying business, 'cuz if we don't make it to Planet Two before we're out of here, we still have a good chance to make it there from the Heaven Zone. (Was that confusing enough?)

Now, bear with me for one second. It's the mix of Light and dark of our guide team, along with our Primary Entity, along with the mix of our consciousness that determines what needs to happen when we leave here. It's not about how much soul we have: Light is Light and we all have the same size soul. As long as we have that soul within us, we are at least partially of the Light. But it's that damnable mix of those who guide us, and what's in our consciousness that causes all the trouble. (You turn that mix into 100 percent pure Light through *Dear God . . .*)

Still with me? Our mix determines what happens to us after we've gone through the tunnel, because our mix affects our vibration, which determines our destination. (No, no not hell, there's no such thing!) Getting that mix to be all pure Light is crucial.

So, depending on what our mix has been, most of us have—or will—experience something similar to what John describes in his book. There will be variations of course; depending on what our intent has been in this last lifetime. And I have to tell you, what he describes in his book is beyond fantastic.

Here's the biggie: For those of us going to Planet Two in either the first or second wave, without reincarnating back here, we won't have to worry about what it will be like to "die the body." We've got it even better.

Those of us who will be going to Planet Two *after* one more incarnation would have similar experiences to what John describes in his channeled book.

The Heaven Zone vs. Dead Zone

Just to put this part about dying out of the way, be assured that yes, there IS a heaven. However that door is closed for such charming folk as Saddam Hussein, or Hitler, or Bin Laden, or any of those other cuties. Entities who are entirely of the dark, as those guys are along with many more, will never get a pass to the Heaven Zone, and never, but never, but *never*, to Planet Two. You can bank on that!

When they leave here, those entities will go to what is often called "The Dead Zone." No need to get into it; it's just not a nice place. And no, it is not hell, which is nothing but a first class fabrication from the dark's clever brain-washing.

The Options of Heaven

You've gathered by now that I'm highly prejudiced toward heading for Planet Two. But shoot, you may just want to stick around the Heaven Zone for a while after you leave here, which could be a few years or the equivalent of a several lifetimes.

Maybe you didn't quite get those frequencies up high enough to get your ticket to Planet Two.

Maybe there are things you still want to understand, so you sign up for Heaven Zone classes. (Oh yes, many classes.)

Maybe you'd like to pursue a stint at teaching what you've learned for folks who are still in the Heaven Zone.

There could be many reasons why Planet Two is not your choice, at least, not your immediate choice. And listen . . . *That's fine.*

One thing: if you leave here before going on to Planet Two (if that is your choice), and some glorious looking or divine looking jackass greets you in the Heaven Zone and asks if you would like him to take away all of your guilt, tell him to get lost and to get the hell out of your way. Don't *ever* give up what you have already learned, and what you still need to learn, or you'll be starting from scratch the next time around.

Anyhow, you get to this Heaven Zone and reunite with a lot of your old buddies who are not necessarily from this lifetime, and get involved with all manner of activities, most of which will probably be to help out human kind. And then, when you find that you've done all that you've wanted to do there, maybe you'll be ready for a rest, or a new experience, or even for Planet Two.

So maybe you'll choose Planet Two, or maybe you'll decide you've done all you can do for now, and all you can understand, and have reached the current potential of your soul's evolution without having to rack up any new experiences. You might even decide to get back to your home planet, which may not be Earth.

Other Realities?

Oh, of course there are other realities, thousands (that's all . . . not millions) of them, mostly of Light bodies and in many different dimensions, on many different planets.

For instance, of the ones we can see, there's Arcturus, the bright star just past the handle end of the Big Dipper. They have one of the most intelligent species in the universe, and many of them are here in body to help us.

Or there's Cassiopeia, the big "W" we can easily see in the winter, with all sorts of different realities of remarkably gentle beings. Many of them are here in body to help us.

And of course, there's the ever famous Pleiades where so much of our assistance is coming from now.

And sure, even Earth could be your home planet.

But don't worry. You don't have to know were you came from. If you're ready to leave the Heaven Zone, it will all be arranged, I guarantee.

My God,
Another Lifetime Here???

Frankly, if it weren't for the influence of The Others, we wouldn't be popping back in here time after time. Unfortunately, all we've ever been told by our teachers of Light is that "we come back in here to learn." Oh grand. "And to grow." Oh lovely. And to "get it right." Oh yeah?

Well, by damn, we have the answers now!

Once we take the steps to rid our personal mix of the dark, our so-called learning process will soar off the charts. But still, why did we keep coming back? Well, for many reasons which you most probably won't have to worry about now. For instance:

— As beings of Light, we felt we could help our
   many friends of Light who had also come into
   bodies. Unfortunately, because of this
   "forgetfulness" thing, most of us got a little lost in
   the process, to put it mildly.

— We were so sure we could change this lack of
   remembrance about our origins, that we would
   actually fight to get back in here. Can you
   imagine? Fight for various bodies that were
   without Light? "Not a problem," we said, "We can
   change it! We can make a difference." Well . . .

— Then there's always been that issue of growth. Oddly enough, the reason so many of us come back is that all the things we still need to experience and learn happen a thousand times faster *in* body than *out* of body. Beats me why, but I know it's a truth.

More about Being Clobbered

To digress for a moment: Remember I said that at one time this planet was so filled with dark that the cosmic bosses of Light had about decided to obliterate us? That's true. It's honestly true!

Somewhere around five centuries ago, the popular thought amongst many bosses of the Light was simply to do away with us, meaning the human form and the two planets of third dimension. Honest, I'm not kidding!

But there were enough of us in those lifetimes who had made adequate inroads with this human scene, and learned how to teach humans about how to obtain a glimmer of happiness, that it was finally decided to go in another direction, and not blow us up. How nice of them.

But progress toward the human becoming more of Light was oh, so very slow, and the cosmic fathers were getting a bit antsy, with good reason. We here in third dimension were affecting the entire universe with all of this negativity and low frequency that we emanated, by virtue of our improper mix of Light and dark.

Nonetheless, we kept coming back, and back, and back and back to see:

(a) if we could remember enough about what was happening to us to pass it on to our friends and families, or even teach it, or

(b) if we weren't going to teach, then just get the message out that we needed to raise our frequencies UP from the low vibrations of The Others. We knew if one of us could do it, many could. But again, very little of that ever happened.

All of this is just to tell you that, for the most part, if you do check out of here, your decision to come back will be because you want to help, not because you'll still have so many lessons to learn. Once you dump the dark dudes, the worst of that will be over. . . for good.

The Breakthrough (Damn well about time!)

After the recent turn of this century, things started to change drastically throughout our universe. The contract that had held us all in the realms of the uninformed was broken, and the truth was beginning to trickle out.

We could now learn the facts about The Others, what they wanted from us, why they were here, and how they manipulated each and every one of us.

We could now be told about their dominance over this planet in particular, and why.

We could now be told that there was a simple way to eliminate them from our own personal lives and surroundings.

We could now be told, at long last, why in the hell we had been held captive by these dorks, and why very few other realities in the universe were ever affected by them. We could now be told what to do.

And, we could be told the truth about:

So-called reincarnation

This universe and how it came about

What needs to happen with The Others, in order to bring our universe into full Light, and only Light

Why we exist in the only universe of Light in the entire Isness

Where The Others came from

What The Others have wanted all along

Why life has been so hard for so many centuries, in so many lifetimes

What we can do about it

What our options are after we dump them

What our options are when we're ready to
leave here

Why the dark—The Others—are so focused
on this planet of humans

Who The Others really are

Why what they do is not really "evil"

And perhaps most important of all, why they
are to be pitied, rather than hated.

We've gotten so much gooey syrup from the entities of Light who have come to try to help, and teach, and push us through all of this, particularly in the last two decades, if we could bottle it, it would sell like hotcakes.

But, with all of the knowledge that is available to us *now*, and the "Oh my god, really?" awarenesses that are available to us *now*, the grand attempts of these previous teachers may have much greater meaning.

Now most of those great teachers have left.

Now it's up to us.

Now we have the missing pieces.

Now we have the entire broad plan to preserve this incredible race of humans.

Now it's up to us.
Now it is up to us!

Where's it going to be for you? Do you think Planet Two may be a viable option? These next few chapters should help you decide.

chapter three

questions, questions, questions

part I

In this chapter:

Being physical again?	What will it look like?
Family and friends?	When's this going to happen?
People I've disliked?	Is my family there?
What's the benefit?	Folks about to "die"?

A Few Questions at a Time

These questions (above and below) are just some of the thousands I've had about this Planet Two scene. I've listed them as they've come to me, sort of like bullets out of a machine gun. But I'm not taking them in the order listed. I'll get to all of them, and do the best I can to come up with responsible answers. A few of the answers to some of the questions below have been incorporated into other answers. Hope that won't bug you too much.

Being physical has been such a bitch for me, why would I want to do it again if I don't have to?

I have kids and other family and friends. If I decide to go to Planet Two, what will happen to them?

Gosh, we think it sounds fantastic! What do we have to do to get there? And how long will it take?

What will everything look like? The same as here?

When will all of this happen?

I have family already gone from this Earth. Are they on Planet Two now?

I have a relative who is about to die, or cross over or whatever you want to call it. Will that relative be there too?

What about making money and existing? Will it still be the same old grind? Get a job . . . get fired . . . save for the future . . . and watch it sail away?

Will there be a California, and a Nebraska, and a New York City, and an Auckland, and a Madrid, and . . . If so, what will they look like?

Will the Middle Eastern countries still be fighting with everyone else as well as themselves?

What about governments?

What about politicians?

What about health care?

How long will we live, and what happens when we get old?

What about climate?

What about challenge and creativity?

What about religions?

What about transportation?

What about recreation, and sports, and theater, and music, and art, and books?

What about education, and schools for kids, and universities, etc.?

What about marriages, or partners, and having kids?

Will I be able to do the kind of work I love? Will there be a need for scientists, and teachers, and engineers, and computer geeks, and botanists?

How will those of us who are going there get along with those who are already there?

Will there be wars?

Will there be other nationalities, and races, and cultures?

What about some of The Others (the dark) who are still there? Will they be there forever?

Planet Two

What about my friends who didn't make it first time around; will they be coming too—eventually?

If it's really such a heaven, won't we get bored?

What about the same holidays we have here, for all nationalities? Will we still have them?

What about animals, and is this where all the endangered species have gone?

And what about my pets? Can they go there?

Do I have to have been—or be—a highly spiritual person to get there?

What will it feel like during the actual process of getting there? Will it be scary? And will everyone survive the journey in one piece (so to speak)?

Will I meet my guides?

Is this whole weird thing still in the experimental stages?

Why is this happening, or being offered to us in the first place?

What if I just decide to stay here?

Will I really stay physical there, or will I have to become a Light body? I don't much like that idea. I'd rather just stay physical, even in a higher dimension.

But what will that higher dimension do for me? What's the big deal about it?

What about killing animals, and fish, and fowl for food? For those of us who are not vegetarians, will we still be slaughtering animals in such cruelty, as we do here?

What about space travel? Will that type of exploration be going on?

Regarding businesses, will major corporations still be operating there?

Will I meet anyone I know there?

Will anyone who goes there ever be kicked out?

How will the rest of the universe react to this planet . . . and to humans!?

I've always wanted to live by the sea. Will I be able to do that, for sure?

Will there still be ghettos, or slums, or people starving all over the world?

Will there still be shootings, and child abductions, and ghastly rapes, and domestic violence?

Will there still be drug abuse and alcoholism?

Will there still be so many teen suicides?

Will there be as many planetary disasters, like earthquakes, and tornadoes, and hurricanes, and droughts and flooding?

Will there be as many human disasters as we have here now, like plane crashes, and bus crashes, and train crashes, and certainly—car crashes?

Will the worst of my fears be gone?

If this Earth is not our home planet, would we be happier back on our own home planet?

What about the vegetation? How close in similarity to our Earth is it on Planet Two?

If I want to stop being fat, or shy, or whatever else, will I be able to?

Will my body be the same as the one I have here?

Will I feel as alone, or frightened, or insecure while I am there, as I have here?

Will I be terrified out of my wits when I first get there?

Will some of the people I have not liked being around on this planet be on that planet as well?

What is the greatest benefit of this Planet Two, both for me and for the universe?

What about insects and snakes? Will there still be spiders, and certain kinds of snakes, and other bugs that I hate?

Will I remember my roots, or this planet, or other lives?

Will I still have so-called "lessons" to learn?

When will this happen?

Questions, Questions, Questions

I'll do my best to answer them all. By the way, though it may freak you out, you should probably know how I get all this information.

When there's something important for me to put in the book, I'll start having questions zipping around in my head. That simply means I've been downloaded with the information my cosmic troops (usually just my primary guide) want me to write about.

Once that happens, it's as easy as pie to start asking the questions . . . in order to get the answers . . . that they've already given me. (No, I'm not trying to be a comedian.) Then I ask those questions out loud, and simply verify the answers I get in my head with my "swinger."

Sure, I could just go ahead and write what I think I've gotten, but I won't do that without having it verified. And anyhow, my conclusions are not always right. For instance, I might be told, "No, not quite," or "You're off base," or "Right on, with modifications."

I read my swinger like a blind person reads Braille, and know exactly what the entity wants to tell me. So then, all I have to do is write it, sometimes with joy, sometimes with trepidation, and yes, sometimes with disgust. Nonetheless, I believe it all to be true, just modified and simplified to fit my level of understanding, and my personal style of writing.

Okay, that over with, let's get on with it. We'll take the questions one at a time, but, again, not always in the order they're written.

Being physical has been such a bitch for me; why would I want to do it again if I don't have to?

Hey!!! No one says you have to. Going into a much

nicer reality of Earth is most assuredly not mandatory. If you've had moments, or days, or even extended times of high enjoyment here, you very well may want to continue that in a place where those times would be greatly extended, like about 70 percent to 80 percent. (That's no small statement!) And that increase in enjoyment will grow to be even higher as you develop and mature.

You don't want to go back into physicality? Shoot, as long as you've completed all that needs to be done to raise your frequencies to where you can match up with your original home reality, you're off to any old place you want to be.

But if you don't match up in frequency, either for Planet Two or your home reality, you'll be popping back into this reality of third dimension Planet One, our present Earth. And I'm here to tell you, it ain't gonna be real pleasant. You think it's bad now with all that's going on? Well, fasten your seat belt if you decide to come back in here. It will be a whole lot more than just a bumpy ride!

So, yes, you have a choice and can go anywhere you choose. But if your frequencies aren't up to it, sorry, but you'll be back here. For myself, I'd rather not consider that cheery news.

Look, there's no magic bullet or waving of a cosmic wand. Everyone throughout this entire universe has had to work for what they've gotten and where they are now.

Granted, you may have been severely blocked by The

Others in your quest, but the first two books in this trilogy will clearly give you the keys to getting that part of your journey—finally and at long last—*un*blocked.

The truth is, you won't have to be as high in frequency to get to Planet Two as you would have to be to go to your Home Reality.

I have kids and family and friends to wonder about. If I decide to go to Planet Two, what will happen to them?

You'll have to face it: they may join you, or they may not. It will depend on how much work they want to put into shoving themselves out of the low vibrational frequency of third dimension.

And please, oh please . . . don't you *dare* blame yourself if they don't make it. Every child born here comes in with lessons to learn. You may have had the nicest, most congenial, most affable husband, and mother and father, and in-laws imaginable. Then, seemingly, out of nowhere, you bear this child who you can't control, who seems to be nothing but trouble, and who is probably destined to repeat this third dimensional planet to learn whatever he came here to learn in the first place. (Yes, yes, this child could be a "she," but for ease of writing, we'll say "he.")

Planet Two

Why would something like this happen? Well, let's say you and your spouse have always been terrific people and high frequency entities in not only this life, but in other lives.

And let's say you have an out-of-body friend who has needed help in learning the lessons he came here to learn.

And let's say you wanted so very much for your out-of-body friend (who has never yet been your offspring) to "get it," and come along with you on your more enlightened path that you—and the one who is to be your spouse—agreed to help him with.

So you agreed to birth him (this friend) as a child of yours, knowing full well that you and your spouse would be getting together once again anyhow, and hopefully be able to help this fellow.

In other words, all of you planned this before you came in here.

This scenario, in about 70 percent of the cases of an unruly child within a totally loving family, is the reason for such grossly unhappy circumstances. The other 30 percent would be The Others.

So, will your immediate family or friends be joining you if you decide to go to Planet Two? Eventually, some families will be together, but many will not.

Let your children go. Allow them the freedom and the pain of learning whatever it is they need to learn. They'll get it eventually, believe me. You agreed to parent them.

You've done all you could. If you don't let them go now, you'll all be held back.

As for friends? Well, there will probably be more friends going with us than family. That's why they're our friends, because like frequencies attract. Our friends are always of a similar frequency, which is why, as we grow in this crazy stuff of expansion, and learning, and awakening, some old friends fall away like dead leaves, and new ones take their place. Those who stay with you here will undoubtedly be with you on Planet Two for many, many years to come.

Will some of the people I've not liked being around on this planet be on that planet as well?

Highly doubtful. Remember, we're talking frequency here. Would this dork you're not very fond of want to read this book? Not likely.

Would this dork (maybe even your boss) you're not fond of be likely to change his spots? Not likely. Possible, but not likely.

So then ask yourself, why do you suppose you don't like him? Is this person nasty? Is this person just a basic bastard (or bitch)? Is this person. . . well. . . you call it.

By virtue of the fact that you're reading this book, I can assure you that there's a high frequency vibration radiating in you that wants to have answers to the Whats and Whys of your existence, and what can be done about it. Did your poopy friend or relative ever feel like that, enough to go on the search as you have, and make changes? I doubt it.

Once again (and again, and again, and again), what this all boils down to is frequency, pure and simple. If some people grab a bunch of other people the wrong way, including you, then you can bet it's going to be a while before they get their lessons and are able to raise their frequencies to make it to Planet Two.

In truth, your son or daughter who is raising holy hell with you and whomever else, is probably closer to getting their frequencies up then most dorks are. Dorks believe they are in the right, whereas problem kids almost always know there's something wrong, so they are closer to a breakthrough—which you may or may not be able to hand down to them—than are dorks.

What is the greatest benefit of this Planet Two, both for me and for the universe?

I'll take that in reverse order. For the universe, it's either that humankind gets its butt to Planet Two, and/or raise their frequencies to be in harmony with the rest of the universe, or go back to the source from which they came. Meaning, start all over. (Yuck! Not for me, thank you very much!)

Remember, nothing dies, but it may take a while (like a few billion years) to bring that soul back to an awareness of its being.

Our universe needs a total cleaning up, a total and extreme makeover. That's what the Birth will do. It will, in a very few years after the Birth, rid the universe of anything third dimensional (because it houses the dark), and it will screen out The Others from coming back in here, once and for all time.

Bottom line? A few years after Planet Two is firmly established with us as its new inhabitants, this planet we're on now will be wiped away forever.

So, as far as the universe goes, Planet Two represents a major cleansing, since we're the only ones left within this womb of Light with such a low frequency.

As to the benefits for those of us going there, it's probably going to be the most exciting place to be throughout the entire universe. For those of us who get there (as you undoubtedly will), it's going to be rewarding beyond words.

What will everything look like? The same as here?

Well some things will look exactly the same, some will not. So here are the most important things.

First of all, it was helpful for me to find out that everything—every single thing—that's on Planet Two now, has been *here* at one time or another, except for dinosaurs, thank you very much, which are most assuredly not on Planet Two.

So let's start with . . .

Trees

We may not be at all familiar with various species of trees that will be there, unless you happen to be a botanist. But all the ones we know and love now will be there for sure.

Flowers

Same thing with flowers, and all of their various species.

Foods from the ground

We'll mostly be growing our own, meaning the best varieties of wheat, corn, safflower, pineapple, tomatoes, vegetables, fruits, etc. However—and this is a big "however,"—what we grow will be without pesticides.

The inhabitants there now know quite well how to do this, just as we all did long ago before we were trying to feed seven billion people and make some big bucks. Now it's going to be only around a billion (the twenty million that are there now, and the rest that will be going there at the Birth and later). So the problem of blights, etc. will hardly exist at all.

Wild shrubbery

If you're from the desert, you'd want to make sure the majestic saguaro would still be there, and the many species of desert plants, especially those that release their heady perfumes after a summer storm. They will all be on Planet Two, and more.

So will the reeds along the Eastern seacoasts, and the wild Lupine in the Western mountains, and the breathtaking fields of West Coast poppies, and the amazing Everglades in our Southeast, and our stately Yuccas in the West.

If it's growing here now, it will be on Planet Two unless it's a threat or hazard to the existing plants or animals. Yes, we'll still have some weeds to deal with, but after all, what would life be like without having to fight a few dandelions?

Housing

Housing is very much the same there as here.

When you arrive, you'll probably be in the home of one of your guides, or old friends or family. Or, you might even wake up in the house you're in now, with a bit of a different-looking neighborhood. If that's the case, not to worry, one of your guides or old friends or family members will be there with you.

From there on in, obtaining your own housing or apartment will be arranged. I know that's really, really sketchy, but my troops are playing with me on this one, and that's about all I can pull out of them.

Naturally, I'd like to know *how* that is going to be arranged. Will we have to pay for it? Can we pick it out ourselves? How soon after we get there? Sorry, no more info coming through. Damn!!!! Oh well . . . If and when I find out, I'll put it on my web site.

Cities and towns, etc.

If you're a New Yorker, or Londoner, or resident of Tokyo or any other large metropolis, your city will be the same, but much smaller. It will still be there, but will look more like it did at the turn of the last century, meaning from the 1800s into the 1900s. With cars, not horses, I promise.

That will hold true even if you're from a small town. It will be the same, only smaller, and probably won't grow to be very much bigger. Happy days if you happen to love small towns.

Housing developments

The huge developments such as our Levittown on the

eastern seaboard of the USA, where we have hundreds of look-a-likes crowding next to each other, won't exist.

Retirement complexes

On the other hand, the lovely parts of developments such as Sun City in Arizona (and only the lovely parts) will continue to provide enjoyment to older folks.

Trailer parks

Trailer parks will be left behind. Yes, some folks from trailer parks may awaken on Planet Two in their trailers, but with the awareness that very soon, they'll have to find someplace else to live. And I promise, that will be no problem.

There are no live-in trailers on Planet Two now, and there will never be a need for them, as the far more equitable monetary system will allow people greater choice.

The heavens

While we'll see most of the same star systems, along with a few new ones, there's going to be one huge difference: our sun.

It's not going to happen for a couple of hundred years or so, but eventually Planet Two is to have two suns. No problem with radiation (?!) I'm told, and no problem with solar storms, no problem with . . . oh shoot. Who cares right now? We'll have our usual friendly Mr. Sun for quite a while after we get there.

But then, Planet Two will be changing its orbit slightly (don't ask me why . . . you can ask for yourself when you get there) and presto, we'll have two suns. (I wonder what their sunscreen will be like?)

So yes, some things will be the same and very familiar, but others . . . well . . . you get the idea. No one said this ride wouldn't be a little traumatic for a while.

When will this so-called Birth happen?

Damn soon, but no one's talking in precise terms. Cosmic top secret! But the cosmic scuttlebutt is anywhere between 2006 and 2012.

Planned for countless eons and set into place by those of the Light, including the one we call god, this whole Birth scenario is in full swing to preserve the entire universe as well as the physical being we call human. If it wasn't for Planet Two and the coming Birth, I can assure you that in a very short period of time there would be no more humans.

The human . . . the human . . . the human!

Did you know that no other reality throughout this entire universe of Light has all the senses we have? In fact, they have next to none. And I'm told there are more senses to come for us. Beats me what they are, but I'm up for it.

Most other realities don't even have emotions. Granted, at times that may seem like a good thing, but emotions are what give us our depth and growth. And, you'll be happy to know that those emotions will be nowhere as near extreme on Planet Two as they are here.

Many of us have been told that we here on Planet One have to reach "critical mass" as a group frequency to allow this so-called Birth to happen. That's a truth. And I'm also told we're closer than any had foretold, so we could be blasting off very, very soon if we implement a few necessary refinements.

Now, I hope you'll pardon what sounds like massive ego on my part, but I'm told that this book is one of those "refinements." For instance:

— to help lessen the shock of waking up in a strange world *(Yipes!)*, and

— to help lessen the shock of frequency variations between worlds, and

— to enable all who would like to have this experience be able to open themselves to the highest level possible in order to make it happen, and

— to give us guys something *huge* to look forward to.

Those are some of the reasons I was told to write this book.

I have family already gone from this Earth. Are they all on Planet Two now?

Most will not be; some, maybe. Until the Birth happens, it takes at least a couple of years of training and preparation in the Heaven Zone to adapt a human to zip from his last frequency into a higher dimension.

Yes, there are many of us from this Earth plane whose names you would know who are on Planet Two now, but that's in another chapter. And every one of those well known guys and gals has had to go through the Heaven Zone and through intensive study while in the Heaven Zone to be able to transfer from non-physical (Heaven Zone) to a much higher dimension of physical than they had ever been before—in any lifetime!

So, while some of your family may, indeed, be on Planet Two, it's not because they just tripped in there from here. They had to make a choice, and then study, and then maybe . . . *maybe* . . . they could get there. Meaning, if any of your relatives are there, they didn't just pop in like a magic show.

However, right now, you're here and still human, and there's plenty of time to get ready to bip from here to there at the time of the Birth, or even afterwards, without the Heaven Zone stopover that has always been necessary. For your relatives and other friends, there's probably no reason why they can't be there eventually. It's just not an overnight, one-two-three-we're-done kind of happening.

So if you have family and/or friends already gone from here, they may or may not be on Planet Two now. And, they may or may not be coming. Not to worry, there will be those around you who love you just as much, if not more. That's a promise.

I have a relative who is about to die, or cross over, or whatever you want to call it. Will that relative be there too?

Same answer as the last question. No human right now, *before* the Birth, will be going to Planet Two without a fairly long stopover in the Heaven Zone. And even then, it's not for sure that they'll be going there.

Now don't go getting maudlin on me. Yes, you love all of these folks . . . your kids . . . your spouse . . . your friends . . . your mom and dad . . . and whomever. But, this is only one lifetime you're in right now.

You've had many moms and pops, and many kids, and many spouses or partners, and many, many friends, more than you could probably count up to. And you've loved them all.

But unless you let go of your present attachment to the "what-will-I-do-without-them" syndrome, you'll have real trouble getting to Planet Two.

Many folks whom you've loved the most may have left here earlier than you would have liked. Just know that—at another level—you both agreed to the event, whatever it may have been, or whatever may have caused it, or however horrible it may have seemed to you.

The point here is, *let the friends and relatives go*!!! Let go of this obsession with, "I can't go somewhere strange without all of those whom I love, and all of my support system, and . . ." Get the idea? Let them go. They are on their own prescribed path, prescribed by themselves.

There! I guess that's my sounding off for the day.

One More Thing . . .

I can't believe there could be a more thrilling or satisfying existence throughout the entire universe as the physicality of human when it's done right. Now it will be.

But none of this is going to happen for those who choose to just sit around and wait. Like, "I've decided to go there, so I will." Nope, that will never happen. There is much work for all of us to do if we desire to go to what seems to be shaping up as a fantastic place. Free rides are not allowed.

Either mankind wakes up and does what needs to be done, or the species goes down the tubes. And that goes for those twenty million now on Planet Two as well. Yep, they too have work to do. But us first.

Oh look, if we want it, we can do it, and we will.

chapter four

questions, questions, questions

part II

(Man! I haven't worked this hard on writing something since my fourth grade essay on "Flowers in My Yard." Don't get me wrong, this is fun, but so much new information.)

In this chapter:

Making money?   Creativity?
Banks?   Religions?

Home types?   Transportation?

Slums?   Recreation?

States and continents?   Theater?

Life expectancy?   Crime?

Climate?   Education?

Middle East?   Marriages?

Do the work I love?

What about making money? Will it still be the same old grind, like . . . get a job . . . save for the future . . . get laid off . . . then watch it all sail away? If that's what's ahead on Planet Two, forget it. "Been there, done that!"

No, no, no, and no! And *no*! That is not it what will be like there, nor is it what it's like there now. Yes, the current residents make money based on an exchange system, something like value received for value given. But it is *not* a wage, or salary. Yes, many folks work for both large and small companies (not corporations, just companies). They sometimes go to work at the same time and come home at the same time, and sometimes they don't. Yes, many folks work for themselves, and charge for their work accordingly. And yes, folks can get fired or laid off, but as I understand it, that's about as rare as winning a billion dollar lottery, which they don't have anyhow.

Now, pull this all together and what do we have? I have to tell you, it beats me. All I can tell you is that money is only used sometimes to purchase goods and services. Of course, money on Planet Two is nice to have, but the acquisition of the stuff, while necessary, is not a "I'm gonna clobber you before you clobber me" kind of struggle. One way or another, everyone will have their needs met. Everyone! Without exception. Plus . . .

There is no foreclosing on homes.
There are no credit unions.
There are not even mortgages. (Oh please, don't
    ask!)
There are no car loans. In fact . . .
There are no loans needed at all.
There are no strikes, because there are no unions.
There is no minimum wage. In fact . . .
There is zero stress over money. Sure suits me!!

Yes, some folks benefit more than others from this system, but remember, you don't get a ticket to Planet Two, either directly from here at the time of the Birth or after, or from the Heaven Zone, unless you've kicked those frequencies up to where they need to be. Which means, most everyone there had a lot on the ball before they even got there, and all are eager to help out other folks when needed, financially or otherwise. Greed is simply not a big deal there, neither is the need to achieve self-importance. Folks, for the most part, are truly happy around 90 percent of the time. That's right, 90 percent of the time! What's the other 10 percent? Oh, who knows, and right now, who cares? Considering that our happiness ratio, per individual here on this planet, averages somewhere around 3 percent for an entire lifetime . . . well . . . I think that says it all.

Since I personally have no desire to exist without smelling roses, or feeling a touch, or tasting exquisite cuisine, or living without color (Earths are the only reality where color is alive and well), then I'm opting for Planet Two, regardless of what their goofy monetary system may be.

What about banks? If all that is true about money, then is there a need for banks?

Yes, there are banks, but rather strange ones to my way of thinking, because I don't understand the system. These banks function quite differently than they do here. Their primary purpose is to act as a place to deposit and save one's earnings, and a place to receive an accurate accounting of spending and saving. Nice, I guess.

What about homes? If all that bizarre stuff is true about money, then what about folks living in different kinds of houses, big and small, with different amounts of land? Or is this going to be like the Shakers, or Mennonites, or other sects where everyone shares in the commonality?

Once again, no, no, and *no*! It's not like that. Beverly Hills is still Beverly Hills, just smaller. Exclusive residential areas all over the world are very much alive, only smaller.

While there's still "the other side of the tracks," none of that "other side" is at all shabby. I came from the other side of the tracks in Short Hills, New Jersey, and I defy anyone to find a more beautiful or neighborly place, or one with more charming homes.

What there is not, are slums!

Okay then, what about slums?

They do not, and will never exist on Planet Two. In *Dear God, What's Happening to Us,* the fierce struggle of those who have come more recently from The Others, and want ongoing Life which The Others do not have, is explained with some sadness and compassion, simply because I feel so intensely for the goals they want to obtain, albeit unconsciously. They are fighters of the highest order. They are the first survivors to come from The Others, and all of them, to me, are cosmic heroes. Some will make it, some will not. Meaning, some will have the staying power past this lifetime to do whatever is necessary to "change their spots" and finally finish up most of their lessons.

If you feel moved to help those who are downtrodden

73

in any way, and anywhere, then do. But please! Do not try to "fix" them; just help. If your help gives them a leg up to keep on going, fine. If not, let them do their own thing, knowing this is part of their own journey, not yours. They may have chosen a hard path, but I can assure you, they would not have chosen it if it wasn't necessary.

Will there be a Nebraska, or a full United States as we know it now, and a South Africa, and an Australia, and a Sweden, etc., etc.?

Nothing geographically, as we know it to be now, will change for centuries there. All the continents will remain the same, along with their unique geography. So will our states remain the same. . . well. . . all except Hawaii which is no longer a U.S. state there.

You want to go skiing in the Alps? Fine, no problem.

You want to take a trip to the Caribbean? Fine, no problem.

You want to stay at home in cozy and beautiful New England and watch the leaves turn, and snows come, and Spring burst? Fine, no problem.

You want to go visit the Great Barrier Reef? Fine, no problem.

The seasons change (for the most part) everywhere just as they do here.

And, if you want to migrate to another country, you'll

find the immigration laws to be entirely different from here. Remember, there is very little fear on Planet Two, so most of those (for instance) in Mexico will have no need to dash frantically and illegally across the border into the U.S., because their country is now a comfort to them. That's just about the same all across the planet, on whatever continent.

How long will we live, and what happens to us when we get old?

Eventually, we'll be able to live as long as we want on Planet Two, but not right now. Unless . . . well . . . here's how it comes down. Those on Planet Two right now, all twenty million of them, are what we would call sixth dimensional entities. They are fully human, mostly of the Light, but not fully aware of all that they are. And yes, there is still a small mix of The Others in their guidance teams and consciousness. This means there is still about a 20 percent influence of the dark—The Others—there, as opposed to about an 80 percent influence here. This, of course, causes the continuation of negative energies there, but that won't go on for much longer. As long as we keep our frequencies up, once we're there, and have taken the steps outlined in *Dear God* . . . we can be living for as long as we want without disease, without all the "I'm so old" syndromes, and without the need for care of any sort.

(Those who have not repeated the statements in *Dear God . . .* will be asked to do so during their indoctrination classes. Gosh, did that ever make me feel good when I found that out!)

Then, whenever we've tired of being there, and feel we have reached and mastered all that we've wanted to, all we have to do is say, "I'm ready to leave," and it will be so. But remember, this won't come about in an agony of physical pain or suffering. It will simply be, "Okay, I'm done now, and I'd like to leave for another experience."

Just so you know, this step will always and only be accepted with the approval of your cosmic committee who know you well.

So what does all of this mean? It means:

1) get those frequencies raised, and get any and all influence of The Others blasted away from you, as outlined in *Dear God . . .*

2) It means finding ways to dump forevermore as much as possible of the emotional junk you have so loved to hang on to from your past.

3) It means getting rid of your ideas about Karma, which is now nothing but an excuse. Karma is gone, done, finished. It does not exist any longer!

Here's how it comes down about aging:

— If we don't get rid of these things, we'll eventually be leaving Planet Two, probably unwillingly.

— If we do get rid of most of these things, then . . .

— Once we remember that *feeeelings* are what create our reality there, as well as here,

— Once we remember when we're there that we'll still have some residue of unnecessary beliefs (lessons) to get rid of,

— Once we've found our most fulfilling means of work and service, and,

— Once we've come to know the full importance of our mission there, that it's not just to have fun, but to be enriched in the process . . . then . . . we will no longer age. Old age, as we know it here, does not exist on Planet Two. Old age, as we absolutely do *not* know it here, exists there, in joy, satisfaction, and richness of life, not in wrinkled up misery.

What about climate?

In truth, you may or may not like this idea. Right now, I'm not sure I do; maybe I will later. For the most part, everyone will be living in a fairly temperate climate all around the globe. There'll be lots of snow on the slopes as long as they're high enough, like the Rockies, or the Alps, and those other mountain chains in Australia, South America, Japan, etc., but not down where most of the population will be living. So, while New England still has changes of color on their trees, it is less than we have here now, simply because it's not as cold. What I don't like about this is kids in the East not being able to sleigh ride, or ice skate, or build snowmen, or make angels in the snow. I think that's sad, though I suppose many folks who live here in heavy-winter places would give their eye teeth to live in more of a California kind of climate. And what we're talking about is definitely more like the drier California, not the hot, humid Florida.

Yes, every place that's supposed to have seasons still has them, just as California does, and just as half-heartedly. (Frankly, as someone who spent some thirty years in California, I got really tired of the natives trying to argue me into their belief that they had major seasonal changes there too, just like everyone else. In your dreams!)

At any rate, rains are in just the proper amounts. There are no droughts, no hurricanes, no tornadoes, and no floods caused from an overabundance of rainfall. However, earthquakes and volcanoes will continue to be with us, as will those wonderful thunder and lightning storms, but without too much damage.

How is all of this possible? A supposedly ideal climate without the devastation that our weather now hands out on a far too regular basis? Oh boy, I don't say that this one is easy to swallow either (like a few of the other Wowees I've been asked to write). It's all the negative energy that encircles our planet, along with the constant flowing of low frequency energy we emit moment to moment that causes our storms, and droughts and floods, etc. Meaning (are you ready?) that the lack of so much low frequency energy on Planet Two is providing a sort of utopian climate. I guess that's nice, but I'm not sure I like the idea, yet.

Will the Middle Eastern countries still be fighting with themselves, as well as with everyone else?

The simple answer to that question is, "No." The more complex answer to that question is, "Well, a little bit, but nowhere near like what's going on now."

That section of our world, on any of our three planet Earths, has always been a hotbed of hate and anger, and a haven for those incarnating here of a much, much lower frequency than most of us.

Which means, then, that as long as there is even a small residual of low frequencies on Planet Two, a whole bunch of those energies land in that part of the globe. And, as long as those factions remain in that part of our worlds, terrorism will remain a factor. On Planet Two, it will be minor, and mostly amongst themselves.

Don't worry about it, and for heaven's sake, don't focus on it. They've got their own stuff to work out, and their "salvation" is not our job. Let it go today, and let it go when you get to Planet Two. That kind of madness is not going to go on forever.

What about challenge and creativity; you know, the fun kind of challenges that makes us feel alive?

Think about all the things—or, maybe just one thing—that you've always wanted to do but couldn't do because of . . . because of what? . . . money? . . . family? . . . social stigmas? . . . lack of confidence?, etc., etc.

If you still have a passion to do this desire of yours, such as sing, or write, or be an astronaut, or raise miniature horses, or own a ski resort, then, while not guaranteed, the achievement of that desire will be infinitely easier to accomplish on Planet Two. And won't that be a barrel of fun!? You've always wanted to have your own company? Much easier on Planet Two.

You've always wanted to be a doctor, or farmer, or teacher? Much easier on Planet Two.

You've always wanted to be a stay-at-home Mom or Dad? Much easier on Planet Two.

Granted, nothing's going to be served up to you on a silver platter. You'll still have to have the zest for your desires. All I'm saying is that your dreams will be about 70 percent easier to obtain there, than here. And, after a while, even easier than that! But you'll still have to do the necessary emotional work. That's just plain old cosmic law. It's how the universe works. Once again, being on Planet Two is not going to be a free ride. But it sure is going to be a barrel of fun!

What about religions?

Oh, religions! Well now. Let's see how we get into this delicate subject. Okay, I'll put it this way. If it hadn't been for religions of all kinds, this planet would no longer be in existence. Religions have given people hope, and courage, and faith and trust, all of which have raised the frequency of our peoples. (And please, this is not just my opinion. This is from my cosmic buddies of the Light.) Most religions, however, after coming into being, have eventually fallen into the hands of power-hungry authorities (see *Dear God . . .*) manipulated by The Others who want nothing more than to create anxiety.

"If I eat meat on Friday, I'll be a sinner." (Gone now, but why was it ever there in the first place?)

"If I don't bow down at sunset, I'll be in trouble with Allah."

"If I don't do this, or that, or the other things within

my religious creeds, I'll never be saved, or go to heaven, or be honored, or . . ."

To this day, religions play a vital part in the faith and higher frequency of many around our globe. But for the majority, the "shoulds," and "musts," and "got tos," and "if you don'ts" have become a domination of fear. Not the kind of fear we have if a tiger is about to attack, or if you're about to be pushed out of a plane without your parachute on.

This kind of fear is a pervasive, hardly recognizable stream of almost unconscious emotion that flows through millions upon millions on this planet. Where did it come from? Quite simply, it came from The Others.

So now, what about Planet Two? If there is still some low frequency residual on that planet, is it affecting the inhabitants in their religious beliefs? And will it affect you and me?

Almost all of the major religions we have here are there. Religions were brought to that planet by The Others to control, but it's not working all that well for them, and before long, it's not going to work at all.

> People are gaining their *own* faith, and trust, and security.

> People will no longer put their lives in the hands of beings outside of themselves—seen or unseen—as we have done for countless centuries.

People will begin to know Who and What they are.

People will honor the masters, who came to humans to help, and they will honor and accept their teachings, but they will come to know that teachings and religious dogma are two different things.

People will no longer (well, after a while) be divided by religions.

Above all, people will know beyond any question that they do not have to adhere to religious doctrines to be happy, or free, or accepted by a universal god, or honored as the magnificent spark of Light that they already are.

No more chains of "gotta believe this way," which is already greatly, greatly reduced on Planet Two, and just beginning to be reduced here.

No more chains of male dominance in religions or elsewhere, which is already greatly reduced on Planet Two.

No more chains of incomprehensible guilt, perpetrated by religions, which is already greatly reduced on Planet Two.

There's a new day dawning with all things on Planet Two. Maybe not the day after you get there, maybe not for several years. But in the peculiar time frame of the universe, it will be less than a flicker of an eyelid.

To my way of thinking, that's worth working and waiting for, for the sake of human existence.

What about transportation?

The bottom-line answer is simple, which is, yes, we'll have the same kinds of transportation as we have now: boats, planes, trains, cars, and skateboards. But what I just can't seem to get a grip on is . . . how in the hell does all of this happen without big corporations to make these grand things? I'm told every means of transportation we have here now, is already there, with some even more advanced. Now how did that ever happen without big corporations, unions, wage caps, and stockholder meetings?

Apparently all of the transportation innovations that were started on our current planet were going on there at the same time. The railroads, the "Model T" cars, airplanes, and those stunning luxury ships built to cross the Atlantic. The time? The industrial revolution in the early nineteen hundreds. We were into it big time here, thanks to our cosmic forces of the Light, and so were our unknown friends on Planet Two . . . *with* corporations there, as here.

But then, those of higher frequency living on Planet Two no longer wanted to be under the influence of the powerful corporations that dominated so many industries. "No more!" they said on Planet Two. "We'll work it out for ourselves without that kind of control, and without being in bondage simply for the sake of putting food on the table."

> And indeed, they've done just that. There are no more mighty corporations; just companies that produce what is requested by the population for ease and enjoyment.

> There are no crowded freeways, mostly due to the population being so much smaller.

> There is no standing in line to go through airport security.

> There is no threat of infection from being on cruise ships.

> There is no risk—unless you're on a Middle Eastern flight from or to Middle Eastern destinations—of planes being deliberately crashed or blown up.

Somehow, some way, planes, trains, boats, and cars get built much as we see them now, only on some kind of a different—and highly equitable—basis for those workers who have helped them come into being. Right now, it beats me how this could be, but I guess we'll find out when we get there.

What about recreation, and sports?

We'll have it all. Well, oops, sorry, that's not quite true. I have an elderly sister that is so bonkers for football,

Planet Two

I'm not sure she could survive on Planet Two without her Monday Night instant replays. But we'll all have to survive without that, because all forms of professional football, whether European or U.S. style, is banned there. And sorry, so is professional basketball. Why? Well, for the most part, these professional games are organized by The Others to stir up emotions of genuine dislike against the opposing teams. For some reason, that doesn't happen in baseball.

What we *will* have is every kind of sport, professional or otherwise, that is not an unhealthy or violent form of competition. We'll have horse racing, but not dog racing. We'll have tennis, but not boxing. Beginning to get the idea?

Planet Two is just not a planet of around-the-globe violence, like we are now. Those sports that emit huge feelings and low vibrational negative waves of "kill 'em," which is so very much a part of our many cultures today, are gone. It's that simple.

Rock climbing, boating, skiing or snow boarding, golfing, even gymnastics or whatever else that is not cut-throat is the norm and highly admired for those who engage. And by the way, bull fights are also a "no-no" there.

One more "by the way . . ." the Olympics thrive on Planet Two.

What about theater, and music, and books, and all of the other arts?

The arts are flourishing on Planet Two, and will continue to expand, particularly as more and more of us from here . . . go there. Remember though, we're going to be the new kids on the block. While most of the inhabitants know this Birth thing is in the offing, and there will be a lot more people coming to share their world, none of them know exactly what to expect. They are curious as to what we'll bring with us. Well, we'll be bringing a lot.

These folk treasure their arts. They deeply treasure the theater, and symphony orchestras, and opera, and any exciting new artists, pop or classical. They have a great respect for competent authors who, even in fiction, have written to make a difference.

Violence in TV and movies is 80 percent less there than here. Wouldn't you know, that's just the difference in the influence of The Others there from here. The day will come when there will be no violence in computer games, or comic books, or toys, or anything else.

Pop singers and groups who are not of rock and roll, but of a more lyrical flavor, are beloved there. Rock and roll or anything at all similar does not exist and never will, for it comes from an entirely different frequency, brilliantly manipulated by The Others.

✧✧✧

Well, since we're on the subject of 80 percent fewer trouble makers there (The Others), then what about crime? Is that about 80 percent less there than here, too?

Right on! The USA still has the highest assault and murder rate by hand guns there, as well as here. But rather than somewhere around 12,000 killings a year by hand guns as it is here now, that rate is reduced to about 2,400; still abhorrently unacceptable. It will be changing.

With that kind of reduction, those countries on our planet now that have such a low handgun problem will have none. But we will all have work to do. Yes, it will be somewhere around 200 years before the entirety of the influence of The Others is gone, but most of us are going there to help that kick-in-the-pants move along as rapidly as possible.

So, in a year or so after we get there, the remaining unwanted 20 percent of low frequency energy will be lessened. In a few more years, it will be lessened more. And so on and on. We're not going to have to wait for 200 years to see improvements; just help it along in whatever way we're guided to do.

Jails will still be there. Although there are fewer of them now, and they'll continue to thin out until the last of The Others have been booted out.

What about education: schools for kids, universities, trade schools, etc. ?

They're all there, but with entirely different goals. Oh sure, most of the basics are taught, but so is a whole lot more in order to provide the richness of life so enjoyed by those who live there now.

That goes for pre-school through twelfth grade, and on through the universities which are free, and where most are always eager to go.

For those going into the so-called traditional studies, such as engineering, or science, or education, or medicine, or law, or archaeology, or computer sciences, etc., the methods of teaching are quite different from here. I don't know how, because I didn't want to get into such detail. I just know that with all of the subjects taught, be it in second grade or graduate school, an eagerness prevails among the students beyond anything we can imagine here.

Trade schools are still trade schools, whether about TV repair, computers, automobiles, or whatever. But, believe me, they are no longer sterile, and have the same unique teaching styles as the universities.

In other words, all education on Planet Two is intertwined with expansive personal development which seems to be enjoyed by everyone. Not too shabby!

What about marriages, or partners, or having kids?

Everything's the same there as here, except much more "partnering" than marriages. Partnering is more their way, and has not the slightest bit of stigma attached to that kind of a relationship. You know why? Because churches are not as powerful in setting so-called moral standards to create fear.

As for having children, yes, it's the same there as here, but infinitely less painful for the woman because of the planet's advanced medical technology. And the day is coming when childbirth will be utterly painless.

Will I be able to do the kind of work there that I love? And, since I'd be going there as an adult, will I have to go back to school to do it?

If you're an expert at this work, then your schooling would not be as long as if you were starting something new. Either way, you'd be free to do whatever you want and receive all manner of very sincere help. Because their ways are somewhat different from ours simply because of their advanced technology and social systems, you'd need to be trained in those routines as well as their monetary system, their ethics, beliefs, philosophies, etc. So, depending on what it is you'd want to do, there may be two schools for you to attend:

1) There will be required attendance for all of us at special schools set up for everyone coming in there. Sort of like a period of indoctrination.

2) Then, after that's done, there will be training for specialized fields, and the type of work you'd like to do.

Believe me; you won't regret either the indoctrination or the specialized training in whatever field you choose to enter. It will be thrilling and extraordinary in this amazing and rapidly evolving society.

chapter five

questions, questions, questions

part III

In this chapter:

About these questions:

I have to tell you, all of this is as fascinating to me as I hope it is to you. When I started the chapters about questions, they came pouring out of me like marbles out of a thin wet paper bag. They just wouldn't stop. My cosmic "gang" had downloaded into my field every piece of info they wanted me to relay, knowing that I would find the questions to ask to get the answers they wanted me to have.

There are times when my "guys" don't want me to get into a subject any further than I have. And I can feel that, like, "No more on that one; it's too complicated." Of course, it wouldn't be any trouble at all if they wanted me to get into whatever that topic may be, but apparently a few words on some subjects are all they want.

It's exciting to me to know what's coming down in the next few years, along with all the fascinating information I never knew about Planet Two. I hope with all my heart that this might be exciting to you, too. Sorry that the questions don't follow any pattern; that's how I got 'em, and that's how I'm pulling in the answers. Here we go. Have fun!

Do I have to have been—or be—a highly spiritual person to get to Planet Two?

Good grief, no! I'm not, and yet I know damn well I'm going to Planet Two. When you have that feeling, you will

be too. Spiritual? Yes, I am. But *highly* spiritual? Well . . .
here's how I see it:

"Highly spiritual" to me means being a fanatic . . . a
fanatic about crystals, and incense, and specified types of
meditation. This kind of spirituality, while it may be fine
for some, is simply not my thing. In truth, I tried it for a
while, and quickly jumped off that train. Garden variety
spiritual folk, like me and most of my friends, seek
knowledge and a depth of hallowed feelings rather than
ritual.

Since starting this journey, I have felt the presence of
my source, felt at times literally merged with that
presence, gained knowledge of planetary changes, of how
the human race got started, of what we humans truly are
and can be, and of how we can help this universe to
become full Light.

That's me. And that's the only reason I'm writing these
books—to offer knowledge and a vastly different look at
us all. The rest is up to you.

— If you have a desire for more info about you . . .

— and man . . .

— and the universe . . .

— if you have a desire to feel more of the presence
of the Light within you . . .

— if you have an unswerving belief that these things
are possible, and . . .

— an unswerving optimistic focus on what can truly be the future of mankind . . . well then . . .

— If that's where you are, you *can make* this remarkable journey.

And if that's where you are, you're meant to help. And if that's where you are, I'll see you there!

If this Planet Two is really such a heaven-on-Earth, what's to keep us from getting bored?

Okay, *please* don't pass over this answer lightly! It's the meat and potatoes of why we are going through such hell now. The human race has been set up to evolve into the most important species in this universe. Yes, we evolved from what The Others on Jupiter did, their cute little clones and even robots. And yes, we became their slaves for a few dozen centuries. But those of the Light knew all along that there was immense potential in these creations that could be turned into the most important, the most productive, and the most influential species within this magnificent universal womb of Light (the only one in the entire Isness). They just had to find a way to do it.

And they did. After it was agreed by the troops of Light that mankind could continue to exist, a plan was set up that would transport many of human kind into another dimension, thereby saving them from extinction: *If—If—*

If—they could adapt to the joys of a higher frequency place to live.

Planet Two is that place. It has been designed to provide for humans every challenge necessary to survive and *completely* master Light over dark.

No matter what your profession may be, should you choose to go to Planet Two, I can tell you without any doubt that you will never, ever be bored. Every person going there—from here—will be happily involved not only in their work, but in the challenge of ridding the place of the remaining low frequency energies.

While you're out sailing, or hiking, or swimming in magnificently clean waters, you'll be thinking about this challenge, in addition to your work.

While you're entering a classroom to teach, you'll be thinking about this challenge.

While you're changing diapers, you'll be thinking about this challenge.

While you're doing *any*thing, you'll be thinking about this because that's the primary reason you're going there, to find more ways to reduce that 20 percent of the dark within your new planetary home. And then to find ways to spur our species on, even more.

To what? Who knows? I only know that this is just a "stop-off" for humankind for the next several centuries. What comes next? Well, that's up to you, and to all of us.

Which is why we will never, ever be bored. If being

bored was a probability in our future there, we'd flat out not be going.

What if I just decide to stay around here, and not go there?

Hey, no problem. The choice is yours.

You want to immobilize your soul's progress? No problem.

You want to return here to where you feel unthreatened, and familiar, and comfortable in the turmoil? No problem.

You want to turn away from family and friends who might eventually be going to Planet Two without you? No problem.

But you'd better know that such a decision could not possibly be as challenging, or as much fun, or as satisfying as taking on the newness of Planet Two.

If you decide not to go there, believe me, everyone will understand and there will be no recriminations. None at all. Only—perhaps—your own regrets which you'll have to deal with either here, or wherever your new home may be, once you "die the body."

Is this whole weird thing still in the experimental stages?

Well, to tell the truth, the answer is both "Yes" and "No." To the best of my understanding, here's how it plays out.

1) Planet Two is *not* experimental. It's been operating quite nicely for several million years.

2) Planet Two as a home planet to those living there now is *not* experimental. They've been incarnating and reincarnating there, and growing, and evolving and learning for many centuries. They're a known factor of a physical body operating in a much higher frequency than we are here, and it's working just fine.

3) The unknown factor is us. Humans have never been transported in the manner planned. In other words, just zip us in, body and all, to a higher frequency without a stopover in the Heaven Zone.

The troops of Light have worked this all out in their virtual labs, and, from what they can see, it works fine . . . *physically.* What's missing in their high-tech laboratories are the emotions. They can only anticipate what emotions we *might* have; they cannot predict what we actually *will* have. (How nice, guys, so we really are your guinea pigs?)

4) There's a thing that goes on in the much, much higher dimensions that I have no understanding of. Those entities in higher dimensions, like ninth or tenth dimension and up, can actually see (for the most part) what's going to happen, anywhere, anytime, but they have to go through every tiny step of the get-there process before it can actually transpire. They can't just wave a magic wand and have it so, or have it the way they would like it to be.

So, the future for those of us going there from third dimension into our new sixth dimensional bodies has been seen, for the most part, without too many problems, but every step still needs to be acted out.

5) Their virtual labs say, without any doubt, that transporting us—which in itself will be an amazing feat—will work just fine. It better!

So just pat yourself on the back if you decide to go. You are one hellova guinea pig!

Will the current inhabitants accept us?

This, to me, has been a biggie.

— Will the current inhabitants accept us?
— Will they really be willing to train us?
— Will they allow us in as eventual friends?

The cosmic troops say "Yes," but I can tell you, if I was living on Planet Two right now, with the knowledge that we were about to be invaded by a bunch of twenty million foreigners (first wave) who don't know from nothin' about our planet or our way of life, I'd be a bit apprehensive. We're going to suddenly appear to crowd out their truly precious space with more houses, and cars, and so many more unknowns. Well, how would you feel?

Nonetheless, that's the way it's going to be at the time of the Birth. Then, for the next half century or so, more will be coming in (second wave) one by one, to swell the population to somewhere around one billion, at which point, the door closes . . . for good.

Their entire planet is abundantly aware of this happening, and are doing all they can to accept and prepare for it. That doesn't mean they're thrilled; just getting ready. I guess we'll just have to see how it goes.

It will be up to us to ease the way for them, just as it will be for them to ease the way for us.

Well then, if the transporting part of this is all so new, does anyone know what it will feel like, going through the transporting process? Will it be scary?

Yes, they do know. And that's the gal I mentioned way back (Machaelle Small Wright), who has actually been going back and forth between here and there daily (don't ask), and describes in detail what it's been like for her. I'm told that no one else has done this, but the process has been okay with her.

H-o-w-e-v-e-r! You'd best know this: it's possible we may have to go through a month or so of rather unpleasant bodily feelings to get our frequencies up to where they need to be in order to exist there. Our guidance teams will be working with us to accomplish that. I think Machaelle calls it "splintering," or something like that.

In order to get us there with the greatest amount of ease possible, a bunch on this planet are having their frequencies raised to create . . . well . . . like a pathway . . . or portal. The point of this phenomena is to help us all slide through to that higher frequency as easily and as smoothly as possible, in our bodies. Yes, a base level of frequency is needed for any one of us to get there, and then, a few adjustments may have to be made. Those adjustments will be nothing like what Machaelle had to go through for several years, a few hours at a time. She didn't have the advantage of the portal (and the accompanying new grid system) that is being created now, even as you read this.

Please don't panic. This is just a small warning sign that it may not be all "sweetness and Light" for the first month or two. Then again, maybe it will be!

Oh, I almost forgot. The actual transporting of us from

here to there will be sort of like it is on *Star Trek*, someone says "Energize," and the next thing we know, we're there. Presto-chango!

If I have cancer or some other serious illness now, will I still have it when I get there?

Yes, but hang on. Once your body is in those higher vibrations, most illnesses will be cured, simply from the greater degree of Light, which is the higher frequency. Those who are in more serious need will get it in spades from the finest medical knowledge available throughout the entire universe. Believe me, you wouldn't be going if there was any chance of your not being able to stay there because of an illness that has probably been horrible here. It won't be there. At least, not for long.

Okay, then what about my age? If I'm elderly, will I have to stay that way, even if I feel good?

No. But don't expect changes overnight. Your age can and will be reduced if you continue your spiritual journey of obtaining universal knowledge, flowing out Feel-Goods and appreciation and all those things that come with a higher frequency which are so necessary to progressing you, and the human species. In truth, there will be some in the first wave (the first twenty million at the time of the Birth) who will not be able to find joy in being there, the kind of joy that raises human frequencies. Their age will remain the same, and, unless they decide to make changes, they probably won't be there for long.

Planet Two is a place where humans will be turning into Divine Man (all right, Divine Human) and all that entails. Nothing like this has ever happened before, and I can tell you that it is most assuredly, positively, absolutely, and incontrovertibly scheduled to happen there. So, the answer to this aging thing is that, as you progress, you will become younger, up to what is for you a comfortable and contented middle age, or even early middle age (you like that better?).

Sure beats face lifts and tummy tucks!

Is Planet Two where our endangered species have gone?

Many of them, yes, but not all of them. Many species don't want to be around *any* kind of human anymore, high frequency or not, and have gone back to other realities. But the majority of our most beloved non-human friends are already on Planet Two, having a happy, peaceful time without hunters. That's right, no sport hunters. The animals there will remain free to live as they were intended to live and die, without fear of humankind. Whether they fly, or wander the endless plains and mountains and valleys as their genes dictate, they will be safe from the sport of humans.

Then what about cattle? Will they still be with us? In other words, will we still be eating meat? And won't that be against our agreement to protect all species?

Yes, we'll still be eating meat and poultry, including cattle, buffalo, deer, and all manner of fish. And we'll be doing this for as long as mankind exists. How come? Because all those living physical wonders of the universe have agreed to sacrifice their lives for the betterment of the human species (and therefore, the universe) . . . *providing* . . . they are not sacrificed in cruelty or in sport.

No clobbering over the head without respect for the Life they are.

No bows and arrows in the woods for sport.

No stabbing of fish in the waters for sport.

No catching of fish by the cruelty of the hook.

No hunting for the fun of it, or for sheer profit.

No horrid medical experimentations with dogs or monkeys or mice, or any other species.

No abandoned, or starved, or abused pets,

—and—

No caged zoos!

105

This is only a small list of how we have, and will no longer, abuse our animals, mammals, or any other friends of the non-human kingdom.

As for meat, yes, we will still be eating it but only from the greatest of respect, and love, and appreciation for the ending of that particular life. That's what cattle and buffalo and all species of fish came here to do. Whales were more than willing to give their oil for lamps, after they had lived a full life, but they were never willing to be killed for it, or for ceremonial rituals.

Sometime ago, as I just mentioned, I was told that many species such as cattle, and sheep, and fish, and chickens, etc. wanted to leave this planet as soon as possible, and not have anything to do with humankind again because of the incomprehensible cruelty they have endured here.

They have since been persuaded otherwise, and to consider being on Planet Two and give of their bodies as sustenance for humans for which they were designed. This means no cruelty in their deaths, but in reverence and true recognition for what they have agreed to offer mankind—and—the universe . . .

— without banging on their heads

— without shoving knives up chickens throats while they hang upside down

— without hanging calves upside down to kill them for veal

— without packing chickens together like feathers in a pillow to breed and be forced to lay eggs

— without killing dolphins in tuna nets

— and without the manipulation of The Others who have caused such disgusting encounters to persist on this planet to fulfill their own needs. Fostering greed among humans, which has caused these vile customs, has been and still is one of their primary objectives.

That whole scenario is too horrendous to even begin to imagine what we have done to our friends who came here originally to serve us, and to help ensure, through their willing sacrifices to humans, the 100 percent pure Light that this universe is soon to be.

What about our various holidays from many cultures and nationalities. Will they still exist?

They will, and they do now—most of them. Take, for instance:

Labor Day in Brazil
Liberation Day in the Czech Republic
Eid al-Fitr, of the Muslims
Shogatsu, from the Japanese
Sakya Buddhist Holy Days
Christmas, in many cultures

and thousands more from every culture upon our planet as we know it now. Remember, not all cultures from our planet will endure, but most will.

Will I meet my guides?

Are you kidding? Of course! They may or may not be "in body," but believe me, you'll know them well, and be thoroughly delighted to see them.

What about diseases?

As far as diseases go, you can just about forget them. Oh, maybe not entirely for another couple of hundred years, but the prevalence is so far removed from the mess we have here, it would blow you away. Diseases come from negative thinking on this planet, just as they do on Planet Two. If you've started to push your frequencies up there, and are staying with that process until you're able to secure your ticket to Planet Two, the negative energies which cause diseases will not be much of a problem. But let's be careful about what we mean by "negative," since most folks view that word to mean anything from Scrooge's horrid vindictiveness to being massively depressed. Not so!

Here's the kind of stuff you'll need to get rid of, (as much as possible) and don't you dare tell me what an impossible task that might be. *Don't you dare!* Try these on for size and see how you measure up with these emotions and moods, such as:

hate, and
longing, and
blame, and
worries, and
resentments, and
fears (of any kind), and
doubts (including of yourself), and
distress, and
uncalled for impatience, and
self-imposed emotional suffering, and
prolonged grief, and
holding on to your lousy childhood, and
spite, and
prejudice, and
ongoing anger (Note *ongoing*. A little blasting off
    steam now and then is good for us all . . . for a
    few moments), and
ongoing annoyance, and
stress (always self-imposed, as are all of these), and
dissatisfaction, and
a lack of acceptance, and
regrets, and
feelings of unworthiness, and
a focus on lack, and
an addictive need to hang on to emotional pain,
and . . . and . . . and . . . and . . .

Get the idea?

Some way, some how, we're all going to have to find a way to dump most of those emotions if we want to get to this unbelievable place. For the most part, they're unconscious and automatic. But we *can* get rid of a good portion of them. All we have to do is decide to do it, and decide to get out of the known comfort of emotional pain.

You want to toss that rock at me now?

Listen! You and a whole lot more are going over the top. We're going out in front of the present human curve. And, sorry, but you chose this yourself. So please, just don't tell me you can't do this. I'm doing it, and am not liking one bit of the entire process, but the whole dumping system is beginning to come together.

You have to find that place and time when you simply say, "Oh, what the hell. Just move on. I'm going to let all that emotional baggage go . . . now! The suitcase is too damn heavy. Cut it loose."

You can do this, *if you want to*. Teach yourself how to implement a few "Feel Goods" every day, and teach yourself how to blast out that knot in your gut, and *whammo*! What you've wanted to dump will be dumped. Once you do this, your frequencies will change. In fact, they'll be zooming up the vibrational ladder.

Tell me more about doctors, and medicine, and health care, and hospitals, and retirement homes, and all those things that seem to be such a pain for most of us today.

Medicine on Planet Two is far, far more advanced than here, for two reasons: First, because a greater input of knowledge results from the higher frequencies, and next, because of the lack of so much interference from The Others.

So, when organs go bad, or any serious disease does hit, the technology is such that . . . well . . . let's say it's a serious heart problem. No more triple bypasses, or heart transplants. You just get the cells to grow a new heart. Then, until your new ticker is grown and ready to take over, your current heart is treated in ways never imagined here. Pretty nice! Same with liver transplants, or bone marrow transplants, or even arm and leg transplants (that's right). Basic broken bones heal much faster there. So do serious abrasions. And so does any form of disease. By the way, there may be an occasional bout of flu, but good old colds are a thing of the past. (For Pete's sake, it's worth going there just for that!)

Health care exists, and we do have to pay for it, but it's nowhere near the bumbling foul-up it is here.

Retirement homes exist right now but in very small numbers, and for not much longer. There will be no need for them as, bit by bit, The Others are forced to take their leave.

In other words, as far as health and well-being are concerned, it's all beautifully planned, well organized, and *waaaay* beyond what we have here.

What about the military?

Nope, no military. Not even in the Middle East, which amazes me. No fighter planes, no carriers, no missiles, no atom bombs, no submarines. They used to be there, but no longer. (I'm not sure how you can open the Rose Bowl Parade in Pasadena, which still goes on there, without the stunning Marine Marching Band doing their traditional opening thing. Oh well . . .)

The primary power source for electricity . . . is it the same as here? Like dams, or atomic power plants?

Dams? No. No more interfering with the natural contour and ecology of our lands. Not even for farming (don't ask—I don't know).

Planet Two is dedicated to the preservation of nature, meaning, keeping it as it was found. Keeping it as it was originally created and brilliantly designed.

No more heavy messing around with rivers.
No more chopping down of rain forests.
No more polluting oceans and streams and lakes.

No more decimating of huge blocks of forests.

Well, that's not all entirely true, but is about 80 percent less than what we have here. It still may take a couple of hundred years to fully achieve all of the above, but the entire planet is working devotedly towards accomplishing this. And so will we, when we get there.

Atomic power plants, solar energy, and other natural resources are now among Planet Two's sources of energy, all built in ways that are without hazard. I have no idea how.

What about gas for cars and such?

Cars? Yes, of course, but not fueled by gasoline. That's another *no-no* to the changing of the higher frequency Earth. Sure, that's worked for us here just fine, but do you have any idea what the pumping of that crude oil has done to our Earth, not to mention our air? Big trouble, big time!

You probably know that we're now pumping plain old water back into many of those drained out wells, just to balance the Earth out in weight. But we're not doing it in all of the oil-drained fields that need it.

So, cars? They're powered by hydrogen, and
electricity, and I'm told other things. All I know
for sure is that there are not now, and will never
be, any more gas-powered cars. Not to worry,

we'll have all manner of cars, just as we have here. Big ones, small ones, goofy ones, streamlined ones, and even antiques. What we won't have are the auto races either on our freeways or on contained race tracks. Sorry 'bout that.

Planes? Well, for a while they'll be shoved along by fossil fuels, but not for long as their technology evolves. Many of us going there will help in that "catch up" process.

Ships? Of course, but with clean energy.

Home heating? Most of it is done there now by solar energy, but not all.

Electricity? Most of it is done there now by atomic energy, but not all.

What are the other sources of energy? Well, I guess we'll just have to wait and find out.

If this Earth is not our home planet, wouldn't we be happier back on our real home planets, rather than going through all this hassle?

Maybe, but doubtful. Some of us will have a choice as to where we want to go if our frequencies are high enough to get us there, and, if we've learned all or most of our life lessons.

Once you express the choice of where you would

prefer to be to your "troops," meaning your guides, and they know you are really, *really* serious about this intent to go to either Planet Two or back to your home planet, then plans will be made for you to go there . . . if you're ready.

Remember, one of the reasons we come into physicality is because it's the fastest speed track to learn whatever it is we have to learn. Other realities have little or no challenge, whereas we opted for those challenges, big time, to move us along.

And yes, we may still have lessons to learn on Planet Two, but without the ugliness we have here. In fact, if, when we're there, we stop working on whatever lessons we have left, we'll be gone from that planet very soon. Just so you know, learning and expanding on Planet Two are prerequisites for staying.

You chose to be human, because humans want to know. We are pioneers. We want to be at the forefront of knowledge. We are, by nature, pacesetters, innovators. Because of this, we have the innate power to create what has been envisioned for this universe since it was formed. That, along with our so-called lessons, is one of the main reasons we came into a human body.

Regardless of your line of work, there is a rich and untapped streak of boundless creativity within your being that would probably amaze you. Once you're on Planet Two, that switch will be turned on. Your creativity will begin to sprout in ways that are unimaginable to you now. And believe me, you'll love it.

Humankind will be expanding as never before. The Light of what we are will explode, and you can be a part of that if you want. Frankly, I can't imagine why any entity throughout this entire universe wouldn't want to experience that, but so few will ever have the opportunity. Other realities want desperately to be a part of this amazing wake-up process of the human species, which is why there is such a line-up to get into bodies right now. Their realities hold little of what we have to offer, not withstanding our pain, oppression, austerity, even tyranny. If you've been lucky enough to get into a human body, your reality could eventually be a part of the greatest transformation of Life that this universe has ever known. But only on Planet Two.

I've said it before, and I'll say again: "Not too shabby!"

chapter six

questions, questions, questions

part IV
(and enough!)

In this chapter:

This could go on and on, but I want you to have the broadest possible overview of this place in order to help you make a decision. I have to presume that by now you've pretty much gotten the idea of what Planet Two is all about, so here goes for the last few questions that may be important to you.

What do I have to do to get to this place of apparent paradise?

Whoa! Hold on! This place is not always a *Rhapsody in Blue*. Those folks who have been there for a long time, and reincarnated there for many lifetimes have worked their butts off to develop what they have now against all sorts of interference from The Others. And they've done an exquisite job. But they have *not* done all of this work so we could sign on for a cushy ride for our own enjoyment exclusively. No way! If we want to go there, we'll be expected to contribute, someway, somehow. And "contribute" is the magic word. No one goes there just for the ride. Frankly, they'd never get in.

Okay, that said, here's what's required. It's relatively easy, but not always fun; and it may be simply too tiring or trying for you.

What's required is:

1) Learning how to raise your frequencies, just a few moments at a time, every day. Both *Excuse Me . . .* and

Dear God . . . will give you those "how-tos." And so will the *Playbook*, big time!

The process I call "Flip-Switching" from down feelings to up feelings, even for a few seconds, *is more important than you could ever know,* and takes only a moment to implement.

2) You'll need passion, and dedication, and focus (except for young kids who don't know how to raise their frequencies). You'll have to want this hop into another physical reality with every fiber of your being, or it will never happen for you.

No, you won't have to: go off to high places to meditate, or run off to meet with lofty gurus, adhere to any rituals; you won't have to burn incense, or acquire crystals, or even read any of the books that have been written in the last couple of decades by true masters of Light.

If you want to do these things, fine. You'll learn more, but not the entire truth as it's being released now concerning The Others and Planet Two and why we've been held back here.

All you'll have to do is *decide* you're going to raise your frequencies in order to go. A simple task, but not always easy. This trilogy of books will help enormously (apparently much more than I've been told), but they are not mandatory.

Once again, I'm not trying to sell books. And believe

me, I have absolutely no idea why I was picked to be the fall guy for writing this trilogy. I've never considered myself to be a writer, just someone who wants to know, and learn, and help. But I'm stuck with the job, so I'll push all I can, any way I can. And that includes these books.

What will the higher dimensions of Planet Two do for me? Will I feel differently than I do here—physically?

Frankly, the higher dimensions won't do a thing for you for there until they get a whole lot higher over time. But yes, you'll feel physically about the same as you do here, minus most of your ailments.

You haven't said anything about space travel. Will that developmental research still be going on?

Not only will the research be going on, but you'd flip out at how much farther along from us in the exploration of space the Planet Two folks are. They've explored—at ground level—almost every planet in our solar system. They've developed, obviously, new means of propulsion. And, they're on the brink of being able to go outside of our solar system. I'd say that's rather fantastic.

Will we remember our earthly roots and lives, or even our cosmic roots and various lives?

Earthly roots and all of your lives here, yes. Cosmic roots and lives? Not for a while, until we're in much higher frequencies.

What about governments, and presidents, and/or rulers?

First of all, all the dictatorial rulers there now (20 percent less than here) will be soon gone (and it won't take 200 years). What they have on Planet Two is a world with 80 percent of the countries attempting to be democratic, which surely beats the 40 percent of nations on our planet now that are trying to run themselves in this manner. However, "democratic" is not always a comfortable word or process. So what does it really mean there?

The truth is, that until The Others are completely gone, politics will continue to be influenced by special interest groups, but there again, to a much, *much* lesser degree than here. The USA has its usual political set up there, and governing bodies, just as we do now. The big difference between our planets is the vast dissimilarity in those who are elected there . . . from those who are elected here. Regardless of the country, elected officials to state and national governments are almost entirely of the Light. Note, I said "almost." That fact, along with all of the other changes taking place on Planet Two, is in the process of being modified. Very soon, all of us there will be governed by people of 100 percent Light, man or woman. It will just take a little time.

> The monarchy in England is now gone completely.
> All of the people of the Middle East have their democracies, but are still struggling with the system, since that is the operational seat of The Others on both planets. Once again, the time for riddance of their struggles is at hand.
> The South American countries are doing well, but like all countries, will do better in the not-too-distant future.
> Mexico, the same.
> Japan, the same.
> Russia, the same.
> Most of Europe, the same.
> China? That country will take more time, but will be at peace with her government within the two-hundred year span.

That's the scenario unfolding now. Not the best, perhaps, but a damn sight better than what's here now, or will ever be here.

Oh. One more fun thing regarding governments. The USA folks there don't pay taxes. Governments, both local and national, are run on some kind of a volunteers-whom-we-pay-as-best-we-can method. Some other countries are run that way now, too, though I have no idea how it works.

What about languages? If countries are having their same holidays, then their cultures are apparently being preserved. Is their language being preserved as well?

Almost all languages, for several hundred years to come, are being preserved—and spoken—just as they are now. However, the need for unity on Planet Two is absolute. Eventually, while all cultures are to be preserved, the language will ultimately change to English, which is beginning—albeit slowly—right now.

A common language must prevail to insure the unity of the planet and its people. That it will be English has absolutely nothing to do with dominance, or "better than." I think we all know that English has become the most common language spoken everywhere. But not to worry, this will take many years to establish, even after The Others are gone. Some of us will assist in that process.

How will—or does—the rest of the universe react to Planet Two? And do they know that we're headed toward becoming so-called "Divine Humans"?

As most other realities are already of 100 percent Light, but not physical, they see this Birth and evolution of the human species in many ways. First of all (and I have to tell you, this is a mystery to me), just because those of the rest of this universe are of 100 percent Light does *not* mean that they don't have issues to deal with. Apparently most of those beings just sail along, lazily ho-humming their existence and not being the slightest bit interested in participating in their own growth.

Surprise, surprise. Once the Birth happens, every being through this entire universe is going to get the message that they have more to do than sit around being "The Light." They will find out they need to address all manner of issues, in order to raise their frequencies—as well as those of the universe—even higher than what they are now. Just because a being—or a reality—is 100 percent Light does not necessarily mean they are of an exceptionally high vibration, or dimension. Meaning, while we humans may be the main problem to our universe, all of the rest of our chums out there are going to have to help, too. They *all* must raise to a higher frequency.

As they face their issues and raise to those higher dimensions and vibrations—which they'll be forced to do at the Birth—the protection of the higher frequencies within our universe will absolutely insure that The Others will never be able to return. Why? Because a low frequency cannot merge into, or get past, a high frequency. High frequencies simply liquidate low frequencies. Now isn't that nice!? The help of the entire universe is needed. And it is known that the entire universe will raise in frequency. (My god, how mind boggling is that????) So yes, the rest of the universal beings see us as a necessity that has to change if we are to get out of the way of their continuing expansion. But they also know that change is coming soon for them, as well. And they're ready. In other words, our chums throughout the rest of the universe fully support what's going on with us.

If I've always wanted to live by the sea. Will I be able to do that?

Well, not with the wave of a magic wand. Just as it is here (but much easier), you'll have to earn your right to do this as well as the money, and through whatever it will be that you'll be giving to the planet. Without that kind of giving on your part, no matter how small, the money will be very difficult to acquire. With it . . . well . . . enjoy your beachfront!

Will the worst of our fears be gone?

Probably, because you will have dumped them here in the process of raising your frequencies. If you haven't done that to the point of at least 70 percent of your fears being gone, then . . . well, sorry . . . but fears are a low, low frequency, and hanging on to too many of them will never allow you to make it to Planet Two.

— You can't just *say* you no longer want to be afraid of your spouse . . .

— or *say* that you want to stop feeling inferior . . .

— or *say* that you accept being passed over for promotions . . .

— or *say* you're going to straighten out your life . . .

— or *say* you know that other folks, including your parents, are not responsible for your lifelong agony . . .

— or *say* that anyone outside of you, seen or unseen, is no longer your savior . . .

That kind of thinking—and feeling—has to become part of your past as you start to create a whole new belief system. I'm not going to belabor the point, but if you want to give up these kinds of beliefs, you can do it as easily as making the decision to do it. If most of that baggage isn't dumped between now and the Birth, or even between the Birth and the following half century, Planet Two will never be your home. Not an easy roadmap, but an accurate one. And believe me, fully achievable.

Will my body be the same as the one I have now? Like maybe too fat, or too whatever?

No, because if that's what you're projecting, i.e. being overweight or "too whatever," you'll have to deal with your lack of self-esteem while you're here, and leave it here. Other than that, you'll look the same. Any pretense or lack of esteem, or self worth, or self-confidence, or position within your particular community that may have caused you to have an obsession with weight leading to diet pills, or alcohol, or uppers, or any other type of mind-altering drugs or actions, will have to be dealt with and corrected here before Planet Two can be in your sights. That does not necessarily mean you have to lose a hundred pounds before you blast off, only the guilt or lack of self-esteem that has caused it. Other than that, you'll look just like you.

When will all this happen?

Please remember, Planet Two has been going on and on for centuries. But when might *you* be blasting off to Planet Two? Okay, here's the two-part scenario.

Part One: The First Wave

This Birth thing, which is a transforming of the entire universe to filter out most of The Others, will be happening somewhere around 2006 to 2012. Maybe sooner. That's when a whole batch of the initial twenty million leaving from here to there will have frequencies high enough to leave. (Oh brother, I really feel for the current inhabitants.) So the first wave is going to be all at once. Young folks, middle aged, and up. Who goes and who doesn't is merely a matter of frequency.

Part Two: The Second Wave

The second wave of many millions will take place over the next half century. The influx will be spread out, though folks will start arriving from here just a few years after the Birth, and keep on arriving for the next several years until Planet Two has reached a capacity of about one billion.

That's it. No more. Then the immigrations will stop and the window will close forever. By the time that window closes, no one else will be going.

Will my dearest pets be there, the ones I have now as well as the ones who have already left?

If our pets have been deeply loved by us, and have had cause to love us back, they may very well be there and will find us. That choice is, of course, solely up to them, not to you or me. And if they do come, they may not be the same as we remember. For instance, a few years ago I lost a most beloved Springer Spaniel. I'm told she won't be there, for she has other avenues she wants to pursue. And, for the same reason, neither will the blessed pooch who left me just recently. But I'm also told that my newer Springer will definitely be there, though possibly not as a Springer. As a dog, yes. Once a dog, always a dog. Many of our pets will go with us directly from here at the time of the Birth. Same body, same markings, same breed or mix, and same personality. What a super thing that would be for so many of us. (And they won't age either!)

And finally, what else will or won't be there that would be fun to know about?

— For one, almost all plastics will be gone. Plastic is a very low frequency and has no place on that planet. Plastic glasses, food containers, etc., etc.—all gone. But the citizenry has developed some kind of substitute that works just as well.

— For another (*and I love this one*!!!), no more spiders (hot damn!), and no more snakes. They both are of a very low frequency, and created by The Others. I'm sure that there will be other sweet things that will vanish from the scene, but I have no idea what, and really don't care to find out. With spiders gone, I'm in heaven. So to all of you vanishing insects, Bye Bye! Farewell! Sayonara! Shalom! Cheerio! *And so long!*

Planet Two

(PS: Flies, totally of The Others, will be gone in time, but not right away. I wonder if that's the way it will really be with spiders . . . "gone in time?" My troops aren't talking. I hate it when they do that!)

— There will still be fast foods, but altered, and I'm sure you know how. (Sorry, no McDonald's.)

— There will still be parades, and school plays, and stainless steel, and aluminum, and freezers.

— There will be Bloomingdales and Sears and stores like K-Mart, but there won't be any chintzy clothing stores, in any country.

— There will be many new kinds of foods, and wonderful restaurants to serve them up.

— There will be night clubs, and dancing, but no gambling casinos.

— There will be churches and synagogues and mosques and temples, etc., but not for much longer.

— There will be police forces, but not for much longer.

— There will be self-help groups.

— There will be an abundance of wildlife.

— There will be jobs for everyone.

— There will be spiritual study-groups.

— There will be magnificent camping areas.

— All waste materials will be put to use as energy.

— There will be a united purpose in all that we do.

Enough Questions

Oh yes, there are a million more questions, for sure, like, "Will I be able to . . . ?" or, "Will there be . . . ?" or, "How does . . . ?" or, "What about . . . ?" But the basic questions that we've addressed—along with their basic answers—should be all that are necessary to either get you wound up, or else get you to toss this book into the garbage can. For me, this information has been more exciting than winning my local lottery, because:

— it's ongoing,

— it's goal oriented (like forever),

— it has purpose along with the joys and fun and happiness that a fullness of living can offer us humans,

— it's bringing in the Light,

— it's having a barrel full and satisfaction,

— in fact, to me at least, it's the most exciting prospect I have ever encountered. My god, I think I'd go through just about *any*thing to bring this about in my life.

How about you?

this frequency business

You keep talking about frequencies: ours, theirs, what we need to do to raise them . . . or it . . . or . . . ? I'm totally lost.

For sure I'm no physicist, so the best I can do with this is to pass on what I've been getting for years, along with a whole lot more I've learned from writing this book. Please know I'm passing this information on in the simplest language, because that's the only way I can understand it. Simple, bottom line, elemental. So don't think you're in for some sort of graduate school stuff. Shoot, I doubt this would make it past seventh grade science. I know this much: it's important we have a basic understanding of what's happening on Planet One and on Planet Two if we're planning on tripping out of here . . . to there. Some of this information is mind-boggling. Some you probably already know. But the rest . . . well . . . "the rest" is what will be extremely helpful to get you to Planet Two, if that's the decision you've made.

Here We Go

It's fairly common knowledge (well, among scientists) that our Earth has always vibrated at a frequency of 7.9 MHz (Megahertz). In the last several years, our scientific community has been finding that the frequencies of our planet are going up . . . and up . . . and up, big time. In fact, the numbers have already doubled and show no signs of stopping. Sadly, our scientists haven't a clue as to why this is happening (which is fully explained in *Dear God* . . . . Meanwhile, as goes our planet, so goes us! Like . . . *yuck*!).

Some two thousand years ago (give or take a thousand), while the frequency of the planet was registering its constant 7.9 MHz, which of course no one knew about at the time, humans were registering somewhere around 70 MHz. Not real spiffy when you consider that other life forms in other realities were registering anywhere from 250 to 800 MHz. Whoa! Of course, they weren't human and therefore didn't have mass of any kind, which always carries with it a much lower frequency. (But Holy Mackerel . . . we were that low?) At any rate, once Jesus came along, things started to change because folks then were grasping for greater knowledge that might lead them to a better way of life. For years to come, his teachings provided that. Jesus made such a difference that over the years the frequencies of mankind began to rise. (You may or may not know that the higher the frequencies of each of us, the closer we are to The Source of the Light within our beings. I call him Abe.)

Everything Vibrates

Hang on now; this is not going to be that tough, I promise. Just some basics. Everything that is, has frequency. Everything that is, is vibration or waves, and please don't ask me to explain that because I couldn't begin to. I only know that everything that is has frequency, which means that everything that is has vibration. For now, we'll just call it frequency. That includes not only us, but our plants, our water, our food, our music, our clothes, our animals, and . . . well . . . everything. No matter what. The planet. (Oh, and by the way, no more polyester or any other garments made of unnatural materials on Planet Two. They are way too low in frequency and cause everything from major health problems to deep, deep depressions. Okay, so back to our frequencies.)

And Then Came . . .

Long before Jesus there was Moses who played
    around with a burning bush and brought us the
    Ten Commandments . . .
And then came Buddha . . .
And then came Jesus, along with various
    prophets . . .
And then came Mohammed . . .

And then came a whole bunch to help us out. A big
bunch, some well known, some not so well known. These
guys came as volunteers to help bring Light and higher
frequency to this grossly troubled planet and the souls
that inhabited her. But after a few hundred years of trying
to make a difference, all of the entities of Light had about
decided to give up (see *Dear God . . .* as to why). It just
wasn't working. Sure, many folks treasured the messages
coming from these great masters of the Light and did all
they could to incorporate the teachings into their lives.
Their bodily frequencies went up, but only to about 80
MHz. Nonetheless, it was a major start toward the Light,
and a step or two away from The Others.

After That . . .

After those times, teachers of the Light got tired of
trying to make this all work for humans. They could see

the potential, and how valuable it would be to the entire universe, but it simply wasn't working as they had hoped. So they left. For many, many years, we were on our own, and it wasn't pretty. The Dark Ages overcame us, and plagues. The so-called Christian church became a haven for power, and torture, and domination, all stemming from the costly influences of The Others.

Many beings, who had frankly *had it*, left the planet early through sickness, or wars, etc. It was not a good time. Our friends of The Light had left us. This species known as human, was not expected to survive. But a large number of the bosses from the Light realized the value of the human breed, and decided to give it one more try.

One more try to get our frequencies up.

One more try to salvage a magnificent creation which was in such horrendous trouble.

One more try to make it work.

So the troops of the Light said, "Okay, we'll give this human-thing one more shot. If it doesn't work, they'll have to go, because their frequencies are messing up this entire universe."

So then came the next and more modern batch of teachers of the Light. At the turn of our last century, in the late 1800s and early 1900s, the first actual channelings of members of the Light began to surface and be moderately accepted. The push was on to save our species.

Slowly, what was being called metaphysical books

started to appear. Oh sure, mostly dreadful epistles to plow through at that time, but nonetheless, something was happening. Something was working. The frequencies of hundreds of folks started to climb. More books, more teaching sessions; "it's working and we have to do more right now to keep the momentum going," said those of the Light who were channeling through, or just watching what was occurring.

By now, in the early 1900s, many human frequencies were up to around 100 MHz, a huge increase in frequency from the average human at that time which was around 80 MHz. And our precious Earth was still vibrating at her reliable 7.9 MHz.

And Then Came 1986

Since there had been only a slight increase of frequency in the overall population in the years since Jesus, and only a slightly higher rise in those who were more into spirituality, it was finally decided that a full, all-out bombardment of the Light needed to happen. A "pull-out-all-the-stops" kind of offensive to get frequencies raised naturally, because if that didn't work for a whole lot more people, the entire human venture would have to be written off. No one wanted that to happen, but, for the sake of this one-of-a-kind universe of Light, it would have to be.

The blitz started around 1986. Every bookstore had books by channeled entities speaking of the Light, and how to bring that Light into one's being. (Of course, they never talked about The Others, because that wasn't allowed.) New so-called metaphysical workshops popped up everywhere with channeling sessions for the serious, as well as for the curious. And the channels (those who were bringing in these entities of Light) were ridiculed mercilessly, non-stop. Fakers, villains, money grubbers, and on and on.

Nonetheless, the rapid increase in these sessions of Light was phenomenal. Channeled books were everywhere. And tapes. And private sessions. And hundreds of small and large meetings all around the world with entities who were channeling through their human assistants. It was a blitz of the highest order, all arranged to get our frequencies up to a place where Planet Two could become a reality for millions of us.

By the end of 1995, when most of those masters stopped channeling through their human friends, many who had been devoted seekers of "truth" had had their frequencies jump to an amazing 110 MHz. The Earth's frequencies were starting to go up now, too, artificially pushing up not only the planet's frequencies, but all six or seven billion humans, as well. "Well, terrific!" you might say.

"No, horrible!" says me.

Whether artificial or from natural means (meaning on your own steam), any raise in one's frequency is a passport to emotional turmoil. (Got a clue now why our world is in such a mess?)

Two Reactions, Two Consequences

The majority of those on our current planet have been pushed now—like it or not—to a bodily frequency of well over 130 MHz. And I can tell you for sure, without any shadow of a doubt, that those who have no idea what's happening to this planet, or why they're into such hostility, depression, impulsive suicides, murder, rape, and horrific spousal abuse, etc., etc., are feeling and doing these things because their frequencies have been pushed up abnormally, and only abnormally. They will not make it to Planet Two.

We are *all* having our frequencies raised abnormally (see *Dear God . . .*). It's been going on now for a couple of decades, and will continue to go on—and up—for all of us as well as for the planet itself. This means more wars, more violence, more abductions, more suicides, more brutality in every form. The raising of one's frequencies pushes every emotional button we have. Oh happy days.

H~o~w~e~v~e~r!!!

Brutality is never part of our scenario when we raise our frequencies on our own, in a manner that takes us naturally, rather than artificially, toward so much more of what we are. The un-fun part of this is that both methods, natural and abnormal (which both you and I are experiencing now), bring up un-fun, long hidden emotions to be dealt with.

Ah, but no one has ever won an Oscar by sitting in the wings.

Where Do We Need to Get

The frequency of Planet Two, meaning the entire round sphere, is vibrating at somewhere between 40 and 50 MHz right now, and rising. Our own Earth is up to somewhere between 15 and 20 MHz, and rising. The frequency of the majority of the inhabitants there is over 240 MHz, and rising. But they are much more able to accept the increasing frequencies than we are. (Lucky stiffs!)

The vast majority of our inhabitants here have been pushed up more than 13 MHz a year since we leaped into the twenty-first century. This, too, is mostly from artificial sources and not all that healthy for the average human. Not to mention that it's causing a mess with almost every one of us. All we need to do, meaning you, me, and the other few million who may be going with us, is to get our frequencies up as close as possible—naturally—to where the natives on Planet Two are now. Then, as we talked about before, the inhabitants will take over from there depending on how much "raising" is left for each of us to do. Yes, you're also being pushed up artificially, but don't count on that to get you where you need to be. Doing it naturally is all that counts.

How will you know what your frequencies are now? Forget it. Don't worry about it. Just go to work on it. And how do you do that? The last chapter will help some, but if you really want to get into this natural stuff, *Excuse Me, Your Life Is Waiting*, and the *Excuse Me . . . Playbook*, are your answers.

Sure, we'll all be taking some baggage with us, but if we have too much, we'll never be able to push up our frequencies, naturally, in order to blast off. You can work it out through the *Playbook*, and the do-it-yourself guidelines in *Excuse Me . . .* but only if you have a mighty strong desire to dump, let go, and leave all that endearing, comforting, nurturing emotional pain behind. Hate to say it, but that's the way it is.

The Bummer of It All

Here we are, just about the highest frequencied humans on this planet, doing all we can to attract the kind of a life we want by overriding our lousy thinking . . . which causes the lousy *feeeeelings* . . . that cause low frequencies. And yet, we continue to find ourselves back in the same old groove of "stinkin' thinkin'."

All I can say is, every one of us has to find a way to stop that "stinkin' thinkin'" to the best of our ability. No, not all day long, just bit by bit . . . even a few seconds at a time . . . until it's a little easier today than yesterday, and a little easier next week than this week.

Everyone's emotions are on overkill right now because of the artificial rise in frequencies, and there may be times when yours ride even higher. S'okay. Just stay with your own program. We're all on a fast tract, with no time for therapy or even esoteric schools. Make your decision . . . design your program . . . and do all you can to maintain an unyielding desire. Hard to do? Sure. But possible to do? Oh, you bet!

Some Other Friends

Now it's time for some fun woo-woo, and even "far out" info. I'm going to tell you about some other folks who are on sixth dimensional Planet Two, aside from the current citizenry. I've been learning of this for several years, and because I've been so involved with this whole Planet Two business, the information has been freely given to me every time I've asked. And it's never changed.

My fascination with Planet Two, as you know, started from reading Machaelle's book *Dancing in the Shadows of the Moon,* and has progressed rapidly from there. But as much as I loved her book, she didn't have anywhere near the amount of information I wanted—no, craved—about this place. So, I went to work with my own cosmic troops who, by that time, I trusted completely. What I found out about who else is there, is spellbinding.

The White Brotherhood (400ish MHz!)

You may or may not have heard of this small, specialized crowd. When I first read about them, shortly after beginning this journey of mine in the '80s, it sounded to me like a bundle of metaphysical, hierarchal horse manure. Entities in another dimension (we were never told where) who were a select group of do-gooders?

Trying to help mankind?
Trying to offer support?

Trying to reach out to help awaken those of us who
   might be on the spiritual shelf? *Poppycock!*
Oh . . . and they had all been human at one time?
   Double poppycock!

But once I'd read Machaelle's book, this so-called White Brotherhood gang became a stunning reality to me, though I felt they could have done a much better job with their name, since they are definitely not all white, and surely not all male. There are about 10,000 of them on Planet Two now. If you're going there, you'll meet them and they'll help you enormously. Some may be your own family members, or famous people, or just wonderful folks of science, or medicine, or movie stars, and all manner of various specialists who wanted desperately to help their fellow man. This was their way.

These folks all died their bodies right here, some violently in car or plane crashes, some of horrible illnesses, some with just good old fashioned heart attacks or old age. Musicians, naturalists, politicians (not many of those), or just good people, all wanting to move us to a place of waking up, and holding us there until it was time for us to blast off. Not a small job.

But how in heaven's name did they get to Planet Two? That was my biggest puzzle, and here's what I've been told repeatedly over the years.

Ingenious!

Regardless of what emotional baggage they may have been carrying around when they crossed over, these were (and are) all basically decent, nice people. Since they held a large amount of Light when they died, they went to the reality we call the Heaven Zone and found out, after appropriate "processing," that if they wanted to, they could qualify for this Brotherhood outfit, and go back into physicality with their own last-life bodies.

This was no willy-nilly honor gifted to everyone. And frankly, not all who were invited accepted. For whatever reason, some wanted to reincarnate back here. Maybe they had more left in their baggage than they wanted to have, and felt they could correct it with another lifetime here. Or maybe they just wanted to come back here to help out, in person, face-to-face, rather than in the unseen.

Whatever their reasons, they couldn't do both. They either had to decide to stay in the Heaven Zone for a length of time before reincarnating here, or join the Brotherhood and be physical again without going through diapers and baby clothes. Totally their decision, but always under the guidance of their guide team.

Here's the Fun Part

If these souls, who were then in Light bodies, decided that they wanted to become a part of the Brotherhood, they had to go through a two-year indoctrination in the Heaven Zone, *and*, a re-creation of their bodies on Planet Two. I've never been told of the actual process, undoubtedly because I wouldn't stand a chance of understanding it. But the basic two-year procedure goes something like this:

From the Heaven Zone, they somehow—quite painlessly—recreate onto Planet Two the bodies they left here with. Eisenhower is there (known now as David, not "Ike") in his same body. John Lennon is there, in the same body he left with, just like everyone else.

Then, when the bodies are ready (usually slightly younger than when they left here), and their two-year stint is up in the Heaven Zone, they leave the Heaven Zone and pop into their bodies. (I wish I could play the music from The Twilight Zone now: Doo-doo-Doo-doo, Doo-doo-Doo-doo.)

All of these folks are quite physical, just of a much higher frequency than the local citizenry. And, they are seventh dimensional beings. They own homes all over the place, just as everyone else does. They have bank accounts which they draw from prudently, as the money is given to them for their service. While they get their first home for free, any second home they want to have down by the water, or up in the mountains, they'll have to pay for themselves. About the best way I can find to describe that is . . . well . . . they accept ways to work overtime to gain that extra money.

It's the same with their cars. They can pick one which they'll get for free, but if they want an antique gem to restore, they'll have to pay for it. Most of the Brotherhood know all of the great masters. They know all about the formation of the universe, and about The Others. While they are known and acknowledged by the current citizenry, and mix with them at various events or pubs and movie houses, etc., for the most part they are left alone to do their work.

So here we have two different major groupings of frequencies on Planet Two:

One: some twenty million inhabitants buzzing at around 260 MHz in sixth dimensional bodies, and

Two: some ten thousand of the Brotherhood, buzzing at around 400 MHz in their seventh dimensional bodies.

Why? Because sooner or later, those in sixth dimension, including all who are going there, will need to bump themselves up to seventh dimension, or leave. And the Brotherhood troops will be doing all they can to help that process along, because Planet Two is going to a much higher dimension than it is now.

What They Do
(But Not Always Enjoy)

Someone like John Lennon (and there are many like him there) would be working with present day musicians here to create more significant types of songs and lyrics, as opposed to the "stab her in the back and slit her throat" kind we're getting now from The Others.

Someone like Eisenhower will continue to work with our present day military leaders here to build a more humane type of thinking, and a more humanitarian image. True, there is no military on Planet Two now, but the last I looked, it was still going strong here.

Those who were doctors and nurses and nutritionists and various other types of health care providers are all working with hundreds of us on this planet to help us overcome medical troubles.

But the vast majority of these Brotherhood folk have opted to become guides to thousands of us, as part of our personal guide team. For instance, I have a dear, dear friend who died in the early '90s who is now in the Brotherhood, and one of my guides. Though guides usually change all the time, she'll probably be with me until I'm outta here.

Guides have to sign up for at least a six-month tour of duty. They can renew if they wish, or can go on to some other human who may more closely meet their own talents and expertise. It's a tough, thankless job, yet probably half of the White Brotherhood are personal guides. If you feel some kind of strong connection with someone who has left here, chances are they could be one of your guides.

There's More

You've probably guessed it by now that, yes indeed, we'll be assisting our Brotherhood friends in any way we can. Maybe not for a while until we get our "sea-legs" there, but soon enough. Because . . .

We, along with our Brotherhood friends, are the ones who are going to be taking Planet Two up to eighth dimension, and possibly higher.

We are the ones, along with our Brotherhood friends, who will be taking the human into the unknown reality of Divine Human. That will be in the future when we're all somewhere around 800 MHz.

By the way, the entity that we call god (I call him Abe) who created this universe, is buzzing somewhere around 14,000 MHz! No other being in the Isness, within or without this universe, is higher than that. This grand entity intends for Divine Human to happen. You can bet that with our help (which is part of his plan) it will.

chapter eight

dumper time,
play time

If none of this chapter applies to you, fantastic. And I truly mean that! I ask only that you be honest with yourself, for if any of this does apply, then dumping it as soon as possible will be a huge leg up toward raising your frequencies, if that's what you want to do. A lot of what I'm saying here is going to seem like repetition. "Shoot, Lynn, you just said that!" And you'll be right. I'm coming at these "Dumpers" from every angle I can think of, because they are *soooooooo* important.

Please just hang in there and be patient with me. If there are only one or two Dumpers you find that fit you, terrific. If there are a bunch more, all the more terrific. The more we dump, the more sure we'll be of getting those frequencies up to where they'll need to be.

Dumper #1: Can't Measure Up

I've got them all, even back to Blavatsky's *Secret Doctrines* from 1888 (not for me), up to the whole *I Am* series of books from the early '30s, the entire Seth series, and almost all of the recent books by every channeler you can think of. Unfortunately, they all say about the same thing, such as:

— if we would just find joy, our lives would change.

— if we would go inside and "know" what we are, our lives would change.

— if we would meditate religiously, our lives would change.

— if we would learn how to raise our Kundalini, our lives would change.

— if we would heal our guilts and other emotional pains, our lives would change.

But were we ever told precisely *how* in a way that would stay with us?

We've been told about gestalts, and being god, and how much we need to love, and paradigm shifts, and ascended masters, and auric fields, and theta waves, and virals, and symbols . . . and . . . We've been told to "do it this way," and then "do it that way" until we're purple. All very fascinating stuff, but those things never seemed to change my life, or help me pay the mortgage. Not that any of what I was reading or hearing was incorrect. It's just that the information never went all the way. It was never finished, never wrapped up. But then, how could it be? We were never allowed to be told the whole story.

It took a while, but soon I was believing everything I read, about how "this" was going to happen to me, and "that." Still, no matter how tenaciously I clung to all of these teachings, either verbal or in print, the struggles of my life never seemed to change. Believe me, I was getting royally ticked off.

Then came a cosmic guy (actually, a group) who seemed to pull it all together. He was saying exactly the same thing as everyone else, but in simple, non-metaphysical verbiage. It made so much sense, and those teachings became the foundation not only for *Excuse Me* . . . but for major happy changes in my life because I could finally grasp the simple principles, and apply them. Wow, what a difference. My income increased by a staggering amount. I was happier. I knew more about who I was. I felt more in tune with the universe and the cosmic forces. I was working on exciting new ideas . . . but . . . I still felt as if something was missing. And it was. Oh, it most surely was.

What comes from all of these wonderful books and teachings is truth, yes, but only half the story. The grand masters who came to teach us have done the best they could with their hands tied behind their backs, but their teachings are not the be-all and end-all of how to change one's life, because they were never allowed to tell the whole story.

So please, don't pound yourself over the head just because, after all of your years of intense and optimistic study, you haven't yet learned to walk on water or become a second Bill Gates. Dump that attitude, and dump it now. We have been led, yes, but we have also been grossly *mis*led, which I was soon to find out.

You've done the very best you could without all of the facts, just as I had done. Yes, I had succeeded beyond my wildest expectations with the principles in *Excuse Me* . . . But then, bit by bit, I found it increasingly difficult to keep the tenets of *Excuse Me* . . . going strong. (I was soon to find out, so did a whole lot of other people.)

Often, in the e-mails I'd get, folks would say, ". . . this is go great, Lynn, but how do you keep it going?" And so often I wanted to write back, "Well, when you find out, let me know."

Then I was told by my cosmic troops to write *Dear God* . . . and I finally understood why we were having such hard times with this most basic and simple principle of the universe which stems from feelings. I hadn't been told all of the facts, and neither had all of the channels (those who brought in the cosmic guys) whom I had so very much admired and respected. They didn't have a clue about what I had learned from writing *Dear God . . .*

Knowing what I know now, I can guarantee you that no matter how exalted the human authors or the metaphysical teachers seem to be, and the glorious masks they may put on about how uplifting and wonderful their lives are, without the facts as noted in *Dear God . . .* they're in just as much doo-doo as you and I have been.

Once I realized that, I felt as if I was on a whole new path, without having to prove myself any more to those I had respected so very much. And then it was easy to get back into the *Excuse Me . . .* principles. I mean, really easy!

So: Two Things:

1) Dump all of this "everyone-else-has-done-it-except-me" kind of thinking about where you are in life now. Once you know the facts, and take the ridiculously easy steps in *Dear God . . .* that will change.

2) And please, keep up with the principles in *Excuse Me . . .* I'm soundly back with those principles now, thank god! They will just make it ever so much easier for you and me to get to this place of our dreams, because those principles, when used regularly, keep raising our frequencies. It's that simple.

Dumper #2:
"I'm Not That Important"

This is where you dump the beliefs that you are "less than." And I mean really dump 'em—like now! Yes, all humans have come from a not-so-nice origin. But now we have the Light within us to move us on to heights never before imagined. If you think that the Light within you was accidental, then put this book away and pick up a good Western. The Light we have within us is not accidental. Granted, we may still be a mix of Light and dark, but that is so easily rectified that no more excuses for your rough road in life are left.

Once you chase off those in the unseen around you who are not of the Light, you'll be able to tell yourself with pride that you have a job to do for the Light, because you'll feel it! (Trust me, if you didn't have a job to do, you wouldn't be reading this book.)

Once you recognize the profound nature of that job, both here and on Planet Two, you could no longer possibly believe that you are "less than" any-thing, or any-body. That belief needs to be dumped.

So who are you? The Light within you is a piece of the creator of this universe, the one we call god. It's as simple, and as profound, as that.

Dumper #3:
Those Archaic Beliefs

When I first started this journey, I was as resistant to this new woo-woo foolishness as a plastic coating of varnish is to water.

"What on Earth do you *mean* that we come back here again and again? Who are you kidding!?"

"What on Earth do you *mean* that all things are already mine!? You want to come live my life and see what's really mine? What a bunch of horse dung!"

"What on Earth do you *mean* when you tell me that whatever I want, I can have!? Oh brother, that takes the bloody cake!!!!" And on, and on.

Nonetheless, for some reason I kept on probing and asking until I began to get a glimpse—and I do mean only a glimpse—of what the human being is all about. And gradually, almost all of my questions were answered.

But then I started to wonder why everyone doesn't already know all of this. And if it's all really true, which I believed it to be, then *why in heaven's name haven't we had this information all along?* What's been the big secret?

Of course I know the answer to that question, but for years I could never understand:

> Why is it that people absolutely refuse to believe that they've been here on this planet before, as I had once believed?
>
> Why is it that people refuse to believe that they may have come from some other reality?
>
> Why is it that people make fun of metaphysical beliefs? Come on now, *you* answer that one. Why do you suppose it is? Because it's frightening to them? Okay, but why?
>
> Why is it that so many see death as oblivion?

And what on Earth is so threatening about the knowledge that there are thousands of different life forms out there in the universe? What's the big deal? Just because we haven't seen them, or found them? How dumb! Like a fan buzzing around so fast we can't see the blades . . . well . . . we can't see these other entities right now either. Even in our own solar system there are life forms on Venus, the Moon, and the Sun. Sorry, no spooks on Mars or Jupiter, though there used to be.

Why do so many millions have such a strong need to believe that only another entity can save them? Where, in heaven's name, does that need to give up responsibility for one's life come from?

I mean, really: didn't you ever wonder about these same kinds of things? Like:

> Why is it that people look at you as if you're some kind of freak if you mention to them the new kinds of universal things you're finding out about? Most of my friends—and I mean good friends—took off like I had the plague when I started to talk about what I was learning. Only two of those old friends are still with me.

> Why do so many humans refuse to believe that they will live forever? Not just in the bosom of god or whomever, but *on their own, as their own Self?*

> What about the need to adhere to—or should I say cling to—religious doctrines?

> And why, in god's name, was all of this truth we're learning, including about The Others, taken out of the Bible? (Oh boy, I'll get letters on that one.) Or taken out of the Kabbalah? Or out of any other sacred writings? If you still believe those beautiful writings haven't been seriously abridged . . . well . . .

> Why haven't those teachings told us the reality of our beings?

Very simple. It's because of the deal that was made with The Others. So if you're still holding on to any of these things, just dump all you can, any way you can, as soon as you can. Every one you dump will add more grease to slide those frequencies up, up, up.

So please, oh please, *do* try to remember that within you is the Light of the maker of this universe, and his incredible plan of the Birth. And that you are a part of the hope of every one of us. Any way you stretch it, that's no small potatoes.

Dumper #4:
Rules & Musts & Shoulds & . . .

This one's about dumping who or what's to blame for how you think and feel, meaning thoughts that still make you uncomfortable. Could be family, or religion, or even friends. I was a huge blamer. Every time something was missing in my house, or in my life, the very first thing I'd do is find someone to blame, whether it be people who had been around me, or my dogs, or the squirrels outside. "It wasn't *my* fault!!!"

I've done this with my poor, patient publishers; with the dear friend who cleans my house; with my dogs; with people who have visited; with my elderly sister; and even with my guides. The only saving grace is that the moment I'm into it now, I know what I'm doing and will usually stop and think, "Hey kid, maybe you're the one responsible!"

But why do you suppose this has been such an

impulsive habit with me? Because I can never be wrong? Because I could never be that stupid? No. This kind of knee-jerk reaction comes from lifetimes of living in a reality manipulated almost totally by The Others. And that goes for all of us.

There's more:

Why in heaven's name have we humans been forced to believe such *un*-true things about:

— our abilities
— our cosmic heritage
— our foreverness
— our beauty
— our radiance
— our equality
— our true being?!

Why have these disbeliefs happened, and how do we stop embracing them?

Briefly, here's how this all happened. (*Dear God* . . . will give you the whole picture.)

The great masters who came here centuries ago, as well as now, have never been allowed to tell us about The Others (yes, I know, I say this over and over), so they did their best to get us to realize the nature of our true Selves.

For a while it worked. But then the religions that began to spring up around these various masters were not born entirely of the Light, unlike the masters. While Christianity had its powerful and magnificent teachings, it was also beginning to generate fear, as were many religions, everywhere. The Others saw this as their way to control the masses, and they did a superb job of it.

For a major part of our population, free will and liberty and the pursuit of happiness had been brilliantly squelched, along with all the things listed below. What a great job they did.

Here are just a few things that The Others have made *no-nos* for us to believe, through religions, through family, through government, through friends, through . . . well, you get the idea. Because of what they were attempting to do, none of these things could ever be a part of our belief system.

1: Death, as we have believed it to be, does not exist. It can *not*. Period! Only the death of the body.

2: There is no such thing as oblivion.

3: There is only ongoing life, like *real* life!

4: You are not here by some accident.

5: You are most assuredly not here alone.

6: You have guides (because you could not come in here without them. Not allowed.).

7: You have fantastic talents.

8: You are now a child of the original Light.

9: You may be from another reality, or you may have been here many times before, but for sure, this is not your first time around.

10: You are the hope of the survival of the species (otherwise you wouldn't be reading this book).

11: Which means, you are also the hope of removing The Others from this universe. A big load to carry.

12: You are one of the most important human pillars to make this all happen, no matter how foolish that may seem to you.

13: You are part of one of the most valued species throughout the entire universe.

14: You are a creator god, here to assist in the creation of a new universe without The Others.

15: You are so much more than what you think you are.

16: You are able to dismiss all of the old teachings with which you've been brainwashed, and embrace the full richness of your being.

17: You are one who will soon come to know why you are here, whether for lessons, or to be of assistance, or both.

18: You will become one who can forgive everybody! Because that's what you're made of.

19: You are one who has the potential to go to any lengths to grow to new frequencies.

20: You will never die, but you can transfer to another reality where you can give support and purpose for years and years and years to come.

21: What you do with this ongoing life business is up to you, and *only* you.

22: You can make a tremendous difference: That's right, just you, all by your lonesome.

23: You do not have to be involved with dogma to get to where you'd really like to go and to become. Fooey on dogma, and the restraints, and the requirements. *It is time to become your own person.*

Ring any bells? If you ever thought any of those things, did you feel you must be wrong? Or even might be wrong? Or that perhaps those thoughts were even blasphemous?

Dumper #5:
"But My Fears Are Mine!!!"

Not necessarily. Our fears can come from many outside sources (church, government, etc.), all of which have been implemented in humans by The Others. Our fears have been passed down to us lifetime after lifetime from our religions, from our forefathers, and from our societies.

For centuries, a vast majority of our fears acquired during ancient times have ruled our way of life, even to this day. Just be aware, and see if you can find those that truly make no sense to you anymore, yet are still with you. Neither our religions nor our governments are the final authority of you or of this universe. In truth, *you* are!

Dumper #6:
"Oh God, Will I Make It?"

Right now, a lot of folks all around the planet are saying,

"Oh please, when can I get out of here?"

Or, "Show me how to fix it so I don't hurt any more."

Or maybe now that you've read the book, "Oh god, what if I don't make it?"

Relax! You'll make it, if . . .

The Appreciation Game

If you'll not try to knock yourself out with "gotta do it, gotta do it," then all you need are *just a few seconds every day* of "Feel Good" to raise your frequencies. That's all you need, and both *Excuse Me . . .* and the *Playbook* will show you how, with fun and zip.

Once you've made the few statements in *Dear God . . .* nothing will seem all that hard for you to do, or to maintain. No, it won't be like a "nothing-to-it," but . . . well . . . you'll see and feel the changes. So . . .

— While you're driving, flow appreciation (and *feeeeel* that flowing) to a red Light . . . or a green one . . . or the car in front of you.

— While you're waiting for your dinner in a restaurant, take just a couple of seconds and flow appreciation to another patron . . . or the table cloth . . . or your fork.

— While you're mowing the lawn, stop for a few seconds (no more than that) and flow appreciation to your lawn mower . . . or a stone . . . or a blade of grass.

— While you're working on a report, stop for a few seconds and flow abundant appreciation to your desk . . . or your computer . . . or your cup of coffee.

— While you're paying your bills, flow appreciation
(never to your bills!) to any old envelope . . . or to
the glass in your window . . . or to the postage
stamp.

Just a few seconds at a time. Find that *feeeeeling* within
you that's like a warm fuzzy. Start with just a couple of
seconds, four or five times a day. When you can make five
seconds at a time, terrific. Then, when you can remember
to do this several times a day, double terrific.

Bit by bit (or "slowly by slowly," as my dear Hungarian
friend used to say), you'll find it easier to do this every
single day, as well as easier to *remember* to do it. Because
you'll want to. And because it will become a fun pastime.

But don't push it. Go at your own pace. If you need to
flow to living things at first such as a baby, or a pet, or
your spouse (if appropriate), then start there. However,
the sooner you can look at your birdbath (as I am right
now) and flow deep loving appreciation to that inanimate
object, the more fun you're going to have.

Each time you do this, you're pushing your frequencies
up a tiny notch. All you have to do is get *in* the habit of
doing this, and *out* of the habit of focusing on what you
don't like, or don't want, or don't care for.

If you could *e-ven-tu-al-ly* work your way up to a
combined total (no, no, not all at one time) of five
minutes a day, oh gosh, you'd really be on your way.

— You'll be operating with higher frequencies.

— You'll have dumped many of your fears, without even knowing it.

— You'll find life getting easier and easier.

— You'll find you have more ideas.

— You'll find people won't bug you as much (not even your nerdy boss).

— You'll find that this is a fun game you never want to give up.

Just remember, you can not *think* appreciation; you have to *feeeeel* it like a loving glow flowing out of you.

So . . . Will I Make It?

Once again, there's no free lunch. We each have to find that excitement for being alive. It's in every one of us. And we *can* find it, even if it's just "let's pretend."

Stop believing that you can't make this transition. Dump that limited belief!

Start believing that you will make it, without question.

Ask your guides to help steer you to dump whatever needs to be dumped, and to *feeeeel* whatever needs to be felt.

Ask, ask, ask! If you don't ask, your guides cannot act in your behalf:

"Show me what I need to know."

"Show me my next step."

"Help me to release all that needs to be released."

"Teach me, teach me, teach me."

Remember, you're only reading this trilogy for the facts. Then it's up to you to go inside and, with the help of your guides, find your own direction.

You have within you the Light of the creator god of this universe. As you begin to dump the things in your current life that need to be released, and play the Appreciation Game, your frequencies will go up in preparation for your journey. As they do, know that you're increasing your Light. Your whole nervous system may feel like it has gone to pot. Pain in the body, sweats, shudders, etc. It's okay; not pleasant, but okay. Just know you're on your way.

For eons, we've been teaching our bodies how to die, how not to live forever. Did you know that our bodies were designed to live forever? Now they can have the opportunity to live for as long as you'd like them to.

You are the hope of this entire universe, I kid you not! If you don't believe that, you will never make it to Planet Two. Come to know and feel your importance, and that you are loved beyond all measure of understanding. You are coming to Planet Two to begin the creation of a new breed of god (Divine Human). You will learn how to Source, and to Create, and to become a Self. In all the universe, that has never been done before.

So What's Next?

After Planet Two? I don't know.

We'll be there for as long as we like, as long as we're contributing. Over time, we'll be working with masters of the Light to assist in the development of Divine Human, which could never happen without Planet Two.

While there,

— our frequencies will go up,
— our technologies will change,
— our concepts and beliefs will change,
— our bodies will change,
— our perceptions will change.

One day, yes, we'll be doing "Beam me up, Scottie," as on *Star Trek*.

One day, yes, we'll be transporting in a blink from coast to coast, and creating our desires out of hand, and all that far-out science fiction business. After all, what is science fiction but someone's imagination? And where do you think that comes from?

But those goodies are in the future. The first thing we have to do . . . is get there.

You can do it. Believe me, you can do it. You have the love of *all of the Light* behind you, for they know you are a critical part of the most incredible transformation this universe of ours has ever known.

You can do it. Oh yes, by damn, you can do it.

See you there?

epilogue

To put it mildly, you are going to have questions. And I would guess that to be the understatement of the century. They'll be popping out all over you, which is good for you . . . but not for me.

"Lynn, you didn't mention . . ."
"But will we be able to . . . ?"
"What if I don't . . . ?"
"Can we really . . . ?"
"Will there be_____there?"
"How come we'll have to . . . ?"
"But what about . . .?"

Just see if you can transfer from left to right brain as your questions come up, perhaps answer them yourself. In any case, *please forget about sending them to me.*

I've done the best I could for now. Answering

everyone's questions (as well as more of my own) would be a whole other book. Thanks just the same, I'll pass.

I've tried to connect the dots and make sense out of this unknown reality, but, as I read through this manuscript for editing, I still have questions.

Some of the dot connections may not make sense to you. Some may be repeated mercilessly (sorry, I was told to). Some dots are undoubtedly left out; not by choice, but just because I didn't go there. I know there are many more dots to be added and connected. But the truth is, my questions will never stop until the Birth and beyond, and neither will yours. So, either go inside and see if you can get answers to your questions, or just forget about them until we get there.

By the Way

About the frequencies. In *Excuse Me* . . . the business of "like attracts like" has caused some confusion with folks, since in physics, opposite poles attract. What *Excuse Me* . . . is about is the fact that like *frequencies* attract. So, if you've sent out a low vibration from even a moderate "Feel Bad," that vibration will seek out something of the same vibration to send back to you that will cause you to feel the same way as when you sent it out.

Now, unless you consciously change that with a few "Feel Goods" every day, the scenario becomes something akin to a paddle ball; you know, that little ball attached by a rubber string to a small paddle that you keep batting at as it comes back to smack you. Since even the most minor of "Feel Bads" are going to come back to you in some way, life seems to become a never-ending circle of hard times, or just plain "Yuck!"

If you can just find a few seconds in every day to flip-switch over to some "Feel Goods," that will start to override those lower frequencies that you, and every one of us, are sending out. That's when the magic begins.

Hope that helps.

One More Thing

In the *"Dear God . . ."* book there are six statements to be made to get things turned around for you. Providing you've made those statements, here's one more to add, just as important as the first six: *"From the Light of God that I am, I ask those who walk with me to begin the healing process of my body. I also ask that healing begin for my children and for my pets."* Whether you believe that they—or you—need healing or not, please make the statement.

From the Bottom of My Heart

That's all I wanted to say, except, from the bottom of my heart, I applaud you for reading this. It is more than a little far-out, I know. But I also know you wouldn't have read it if there wasn't a reason. And I think you know what that is.

We're all in this together, and while not a hugely pleasant ride at this time, the effects of what we are doing now will be beyond measure in time to come.

My love to you, my very, very best to you, and from every fiber of my being, my heartfelt gratitude to you.

lynn

about the author

Lynn Grabhorn is a long-time student of the way in which thought and feelings format our lives. Raised in Short Hills, New Jersey, she began her working life in the advertising field in New York City, founded and ran an audio-visual educational publishing company in Los Angeles, and owned and ran a mortgage brokerage firm in Washington State.

Lynn's books, *Excuse Me, Your Life Is Waiting*, *The Excuse Me Your Life Is Waiting Playbook*, *Beyond the Twelve Steps*, and *Dear God! What's Happening to Us?*, have received high acclaim from all corners of the world.

For more information, see Lynn's web page at lynngrabhorn.com.